LAVENDER FOR ALL SEASONS

Lavender for All Seasons

A Gardener's Guide to Growing and Creating with Lavender Year-Round

Paola Legarre
Photography by Kenneth Redding

TIMBER PRESS
PORTLAND, OREGON

Copyright © 2025 by Paola Legarre. All rights reserved.

Photo credits appear on page 252.

Hachette Book Group supports the right to free expression and the value of copyright. The purpose of copyright is to encourage writers and artists to produce the creative works that enrich our culture. The scanning, uploading, and distribution of this book without permission is a theft of the author's intellectual property. If you would like permission to use material from the book (other than for review purposes), please contact permissions@hbgusa.com. Thank you for your support of the author's rights.

Timber Press
Workman Publishing
Hachette Book Group, Inc.
1290 Avenue of the Americas
New York, New York 10104
timberpress.com

Timber Press is an imprint of Workman Publishing, a division of Hachette Book Group, Inc. The Timber Press name and logo are registered trademarks of Hachette Book Group, Inc.

Printed in China on responsibly sourced paper

Text and cover design by Brooke Johnson

The publisher is not responsible for websites (or their content) that are not owned by the publisher.

The Hachette Speakers Bureau provides a wide range of authors for speaking events. To find out more, go to hachettespeakersbureau.com or email hachettespeakers@hbgusa.com.

ISBN 978-1-64326-186-7

A catalog record for this book is available from the Library of Congress.

To my grandmother Anna R., who encouraged
me to roam free in the garden

To my dearest Bobby, Anna, and Sophia, my patient
family, who support my lavender passion

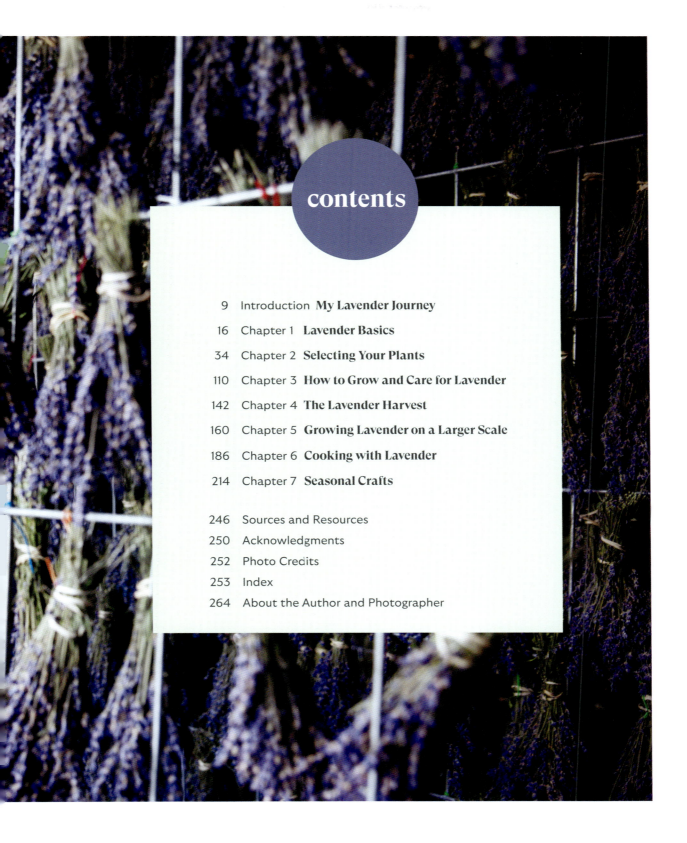

contents

- 9 — Introduction **My Lavender Journey**
- 16 — Chapter 1 **Lavender Basics**
- 34 — Chapter 2 **Selecting Your Plants**
- 110 — Chapter 3 **How to Grow and Care for Lavender**
- 142 — Chapter 4 **The Lavender Harvest**
- 160 — Chapter 5 **Growing Lavender on a Larger Scale**
- 186 — Chapter 6 **Cooking with Lavender**
- 214 — Chapter 7 **Seasonal Crafts**

- 246 — Sources and Resources
- 250 — Acknowledgments
- 252 — Photo Credits
- 253 — Index
- 264 — About the Author and Photographer

My Lavender Journey

LIFE IS FUNNY, THE WAY IT WENDS, when small moments and unexpected bits of experience somehow coalesce into a path, into meaning, and into beauty. Looking back, I see that the meandering path I followed to arrive at farming lavender makes perfect sense.

The plant world entered my life at an early age. Poignant memories of the sweet scent of orange blossoms wafting in through the kitchen window, the resinous smell of green walnuts in their husks, and the invigorating aroma of wild mint on my grandmother's small farm are embedded in my childhood.

I spent many summers on her farm in California's northern San Joaquin Valley. She was surrounded by ancient vineyards and orchards; her garden was filled with nut trees, citrus, and grapes. Her soil was so sandy that in the blazing summer months, it was often a too-hot beach to my ever-present bare feet, necessitating a sprint across the fields to find relief in the nearby ditches or furrows brimming with cold irrigation water. Seeking reprieve from the long, hot summer days, I would venture to the cellar, where "Just Married" was still written in chalk on the cement wall from the day in 1932 when my grandmother, Anna, married my grandfather, Gabe. The cellar shelves were filled with a rainbow of jars of canned and fermented vegetables and fruits such as tomatoes, peaches, apricots, and sauerkraut from my grandmother's garden. I think it was the transformation and the gift each jar held that so awed and captivated me—the burgeoning trees, vines, and stalks growing in the soil above and now the harvest stored here, patiently waiting in the cool dark. It seemed like magic.

Years later, while I was working on farms along the northern California coast and in the Sacramento Valley, it was the daily packing shed ambience of fresh-cut herbs and earth, the smell of heirloom tomatoes, ripe melons, and freshly harvested

Paola on her farm, in the drying room.

garlic getting ready for market that captivated me. It was these moments, these experiences, that I now see brought me to lavender.

A memory I cannot forget is of a family friend in St. Helena, California, who landscaped her front yard on a residential block with lavender. The lawn was removed and replaced with 'Provence', a lovely cultivar that has light purple flowers. The area was enclosed with a white picket fence and filled with small rows of alternately spaced lavender plants. When I visited, the long waving stems carried large flower heads in full bloom. She invited me to cut a few bundles to take with me. When I returned home, I dried the bundles, removed the buds over a newspaper, and then placed them in a bowl. The natural perfume of those buds lingered in my home for months. The smell and sensation were so pleasant, transporting me back in time to her beautiful garden.

At that time, I never had the thought *one day I am going to grow lavender and write a book about it*. Yet I catalog that memory as one of many that led me to lavender, to where I am today. The simple tactile and sensory memory of that moment is engraved in my body. This happened almost ten years before I started growing lavender in Colorado. From the magical farm of my girlhood through to this very day here on my own, these simple, memorable experiences with plants and nature have somehow accumulated inside me, have become indelible, and have become a part of who I am. Experiences of scent, texture, light, and transformation hold on and have the power to lead one to a destiny one never would have imagined or predicted.

Plants and their bounty always intrigued me. But my vocation was not intentional in the beginning; it grew over time. The joy of farming and gardening evolved with the fragrances, textures, and colors of the plants I grew and touched. I observed which insects were attracted to certain plants, why that matters, and how the plant made me feel when I was among its canopy or working with its flora or fruit.

In the beginning I had the simple inspiration of growing forty plants just to see if lavender would thrive at our new home in Palisade, Colorado, here in the high desert at an elevation of 4800 feet. Now I have more than nineteen thousand plants and more than sixty-five cultivars, and I am farming ten acres, six acres of which are in lavender.

I founded my farm, Sage Creations, in 2006, after more than fifteen years of working in agriculture and when my husband and I had recently had our first daughter. The desire to be present and hands-on in her life (and in our soon-to-arrive second daughter's life) shaped the way we grew our farm: slowly and patiently. Meanwhile, our girls grew up paying attention to seasons, ebbing and flowing with the yearly rhythm of farming and its seasonal tasks, and enjoying the fruits of our labor. They grew up watching plants grow from cuttings and seeds, seeing greenhouses built and cherry trees marked for sugar content, watered, and harvested. They grew up chasing a woman on a mission.

Sage Creations has grown into a family farm where we now welcome visitors, hold classes, propagate a long list of different lavender cultivars, create balms with our farm-distilled essential oils, and arrange bouquets and wreaths using our dried and fresh lavender. Our lavender fields slowly expanded. Our forty plants became a row, which turned into a patch, then a field, and now a crop rotation of six acres at any given time. Along the way I experimented with my crops—cooking, distilling, arranging—and became familiar with every small detail of how the plant behaved and performed in whatever creation I was making at the time. I infused each true lavender (*Lavandula angustifolia*) I grew into a simple syrup, attempted to use lavandins (*Lavandula ×intermedia*) in extracts and tinctures, and distilled many different cultivars to see which I found the most aromatic and chemically complete for aromatherapy. I harvested and dried every different type of lavender to see which one held its color and form the best. I propagated all sixty-five cultivars I was growing to see which ones would root easily and which ones required

Close-up of *Lavandula angustifolia*

Close-up of *Lavandula* ×*intermedia*

trialing over and over again until I somehow got it just right. My experiences and research have allowed me to share my knowledge with countless gardeners and growers around the world. My desire to learn the entirety of what the plant has to offer has gifted me this wealth of experience. I now wish to share it with you.

The offerings in this book come from hands-on experience. Here I share my knowledge of the small and large details of growing and creating with this most amazing plant. I aim to teach and show you how to incorporate lavender in your everyday life throughout the seasons, whether in the garden, in your home, in your cooking, or on your body. In the pages ahead, you will find all the information you need to start growing and creating with lavender.

The book covers plant selection first, then moves on to growing lavender, and finally describes culinary and craft applications. Chapter 1 lays out the basics of lavender: its history, its botany and chemistry, its uses. Chapter 2 focuses on helping you select lavender to grow based on your climate, desired colors, and intended uses. It provides a comprehensive overview of plants that make for an excellent lavender garden or farm. Chapters 3 and 4 contain tips on how to care for and maintain your lavender plants and how to harvest and process your lavender flowers. I have dedicated chapter 5 to techniques for scaling up planting beyond the garden setting, and thoughts on how to establish and transform your available space into anything from a small patch to a large production field of lavender. Chapters 6 and 7 offer recipes and crafts that follow the seasons of the year. There you will discover how to integrate lavender into your apothecary, your pantry, and your crafting space.

Rest assured, whether you're growing one plant or a thousand, the book addresses concerns at all levels of experience and scale. I have included a multitude of hints, tips, and personal lessons learned. These tips can be read as the textbook from my School of Farmer's Hard Knocks—those lessons I had to learn through making mistakes, starting over, and trying again and again.

I wrote this book for you. If you are holding it in your hands, I suspect you are curious about lavender. Whether you are a novice who is ready to take your first steps along the path, a budding commercial grower who wants in-depth information and insights, or a lavender fan at any point in between, this book is meant for you. Above all else, I hope to inspire you to grow lavender and embark on your own lavender journey. I hope yours will be as transformative, captivating, and awe-filled as mine has been. I look forward to seeing you on the path!

Chapter 1

Lavender Basics

For thousands of years, cultures around the globe have harnessed the powerful properties of lavender. This prized herb has been used throughout the centuries in a myriad of ways. In ancient Egypt, lavender was used in the mummification process; in ancient Rome, dried lavender was scattered on the floors of field hospitals to deodorize and absorb fluids, and lavender scented the water in public bathhouses. Lavender found medicinal and culinary uses in medieval Europe, and dried lavender covered castle floors.

Lavender is just as useful and captivating now as it was then. It lends its scent to cleaning products and clothes-dryer bags, bath salts and soaps and lotions. Its use in aromatherapy to induce relaxation is well known. Rarely do I encounter a visitor to our farm during lavender bloom who doesn't feel a deep sense of calm while walking the gardens and fields. And with its lovely hues of purple and pink, it accents garden borders and makes a fragrant cut display bunched in vases indoors.

Purple spikes of lavender line a garden path in late summer, complementing the colors of sedum, red orache, and coneflower in the border.

Lavender Then and Now

Lavender is mentioned throughout more than twenty-five hundred years of recorded history, yet its exact origin remains a mystery. Some species are thought to have been domesticated in Arabia originally. The plant may have traveled with Greek traders as far back as 600 BCE to what are now known as the Hyères Islands off the southern coast of France and spread to areas we now know as France, Italy, and Spain. The first recorded arrival of the plant on the North American continent dates to the 1600s. At the turn of the nineteenth century, England became known as the producer of the "sweetest" of the oils, and France was (and still is) famous for its production of essential oil from various species of lavender for fragrances, perfumes, and cleaning products. European artists used lavender essential oil to thin their oil paints.

Since those times, lavender has crossed the continents from Europe, and its production has flourished on a global level. Rolling hills of lavender and some of the largest fields in the world can be found in Japan. The purple revolution has migrated to the arid regions of Kashmir in the Indian subcontinent, where small farmers have converted their maize fields to lavender. Lavender is now cultivated and processed in North America, Mexico, South America, western and eastern Europe, the Asia-Pacific region, the Middle East, Japan, Australia, New Zealand,

South Africa, China, Turkey, and India. Bulgaria is the largest producer of lavender for essential oil in the world, with fields covering more than sixty-five square miles. Second to Bulgaria in production is France, then China. You will find lavender blooming in some corner of the world in every season of the year.

Our blooming commercial field in Colorado.

LAVENDER BASICS 19

Lavender in the Garden, Kitchen, and Apothecary

As the farm's flora awakens from the shortest days of the year in late winter and early spring, we begin to work with herbs and lavender plants in our greenhouses. The mint perks up first, then the costmary, yarrow, chives, and parsley, and later the lavender. All these common herbs were also found in monastic gardens during medieval times. To warm our bodies and lighten our step throughout the short days of winter, I and my three friends whom I call the trusted sisters brew a tea of dried herbs from the previous season's harvest, or we snip newly emerging leaves in the hoop house to add flavor to our lunch plates.

To think these same herbs were used by Hildegard of Bingen (1098–1179), a German abbess, prophet, herbalist, and composer, creates visions in my mind of an enchanted time. Hildegard wrote extensively of the healing properties of plants and noted in her volume *Physica* (translated from the Latin by Priscilla Throop):

What's in a Name?

I use Latin names for lavender rather than common names, because common names can sometimes create confusion. Common names can differ from place to place, and many plants have more than one common name. For example, *Lavandula stoechas* is often referred to as Spanish lavender in the United States and French lavender in the United Kingdom. At the same time, the hybrid cross *Lavandula ×intermedia* is generally called French lavender in the United States. Referring to lavenders as English, French, or Spanish is bewildering; none of these names are true, and all are best avoided. I have learned that using the Latin names for species and subspecies ensures we are all speaking the same language, no matter where we live.

Latin names can be abbreviated like this: *L. angustifolia*, *L. ×intermedia*. Names of cultivars, or cultivated varieties, are in single quotes and capitalized—for example, *Lavandula angustifolia* 'Folgate'.

Hybrids are given unique names preceded with an ×, indicating that this plant is a cross between two species. Unfortunately, this doesn't tell us which two species; you would never know that *Lavandula ×intermedia* is a hybrid of *L. angustifolia* and *L. latifolia*.

Whoever cooks lavender in wine, or if the person has no wine, with honey and water, and drinks it when it is warm, will lessen the pain in his liver and lungs, and the stiffness in his chest. It also makes his thinking and disposition pure.

In your own garden, you may have grown plants in the mint family (Lamiaceae). Many of these plants are culinary favorites, including basil, sage, rosemary, and thyme. These herbs, which are related to lavender not only in their botany but also in their scent (woodsy, piney, and sweet), are a great way into growing the plant. My first gardens and early farm work included extensive experience with these herbs. I long ago began to appreciate the versatility and ease of growing them, and lavender naturally followed. Lavender's membership in the mint family explains its versatility and its many healing powers.

If you encounter a plant with a distinctly square stalk, simple leaves growing opposite each other, and two-lipped open-mouthed tubular flowers, it is very likely a member of the mint family. Worldwide there are about 180 genera in this family, representing some 3500 species. Approximately 50 of these genera are found in North America. The genus *Lavandula* (lavender) belongs to the mint family and includes more than forty flowering species originating from countries bordering the Mediterranean Sea and southern Europe, northern Africa, and western Asia. Only a few species have herbal uses and are commercially grown for the manufacture of essential oil. Among them are *Lavandula angustifolia* (true lavender), *Lavandula ×intermedia* (lavandin), and *Lavandula latifolia* (spike lavender).

Various species of the genus *Lavandula* have been used for centuries in aromatic and medicinal products. The essential oil from *Lavandula* is known to have a wide range of biological activities, including antimicrobial, anxiety-reduction, anti-inflammatory, and antioxidant properties. *Lavandula angustifolia* is used in pharmaceuticals and aromatherapy as one of the most popular herbal remedies for treating conditions such as stress, anxiety, depression, and sleep disorders.

Lavender Anatomy

Understanding the anatomy of lavender will help you grasp where its benefits come from. Although different species and cultivars of lavender vary widely in appearance, with a vast range of flower and foliage colors and flower head sizes and shapes, all the basic parts are the same.

THE FLOWER SPIKE

Lavender's flowering shoot, or inflorescence, is known as the *spike*. On closer inspection, you can see that each spike consists of clusters of flowers (*cymes*) arranged around the central stem in whorls (*verticillasters*). The gap between these whorls can vary among species and can be uneven. Cymes flower sequentially due to their structure, resulting in flowers blooming over a long period of time. In each cyme, the first flower to open is in the middle, and then flowering proceeds from the middle outward. Different cultivars may have different numbers of flowers per cyme, and this number can vary from the top to the bottom of the flowering shoot on the same plant. There is typically one verticillaster at a greater distance below the others on a spike, known as the *remote verticillaster*.

Look more closely still and you will see that in all types of lavender, each flower in a cyme is composed of two major parts: the *calyx* (bud or sepals) and the *corolla* (or petals). The corolla tube emerges from the calyx to display five lobes, two at

Lavandula angustifolia and *Lavandula stoechas* flower spikes in spring and summer display an array of shades of blue, purple, white, and pink.

Anatomy of a flower spike from *Lavandula angustifolia* 'Seals Seven Oaks'.

Anatomy of a flower spike from *Lavandula stoechas*.

the top and three at the bottom. Oftentimes with the naked eye you can see calyxes covered with fine glandular hairs, known as *woolly indumentum*, that contain and secrete aromatic essential oils.

In most lavenders, tiny green *bracts* cradle each of the flower clusters or cymes. *Lavandula stoechas* cultivars have a unique feature on top of their flower heads—*apical bracts* often called wings or rabbit ears. Because the true blossoms are so small, the flashy purple or dark violet bracts are sometimes mistaken for petals.

The calyx is where the essential oil glands reside. In steam distilling, these glands burst open and release the essential oil. This is the main source of most of the aromatic oils responsible for the beneficial scents and the majority of chemical compounds that both humans and pollinators find so appealing. In *Lavandula angustifolia* and *Lavandula ×intermedia*, the most valuable part of the plant is the flowers, due to their much higher essential oil content than the leaves. *Lavandula stoechas* is mainly used ornamentally and not for its oil.

THE STEM AND LEAF

Leaves and stems (*peduncles*) can vary widely among lavender species and cultivars. Leaves vary in shape, size, and color. The leaves are arranged opposite each other on the stem, and the inflorescence develops from the *axil* of each leaf (the junction between the leaf and the stem). Besides the central stem and flower spike, there are lateral branches or secondary spikes, more pronounced visually in some species than in others. The lateral branches appear in one, two, or three pairs, depending on the cultivar.

Stem length, measured from the base of the spike to the start of the foliage, can make a lavender shrub seem tight and compact or can cause the blooms to be held far above waist height. Stems can be straight and upright, wavy, or semi-wavy; they can be thick or thin. Variations can depend on growing conditions, species, and cultivar. Some cultivars' stems shatter more easily than others', making some cultivars better than others for crafting.

VARIATIONS AMONG SPECIES

Comparing the characteristic features of *Lavandula angustifolia* with those of *Lavandula ×intermedia* illustrates variations in lavender anatomy. Lavandins are bigger plants with larger flowers than true lavender, and the flower spikes of lavandins are much taller than those of true lavender. In *L. angustifolia*, the stem branches from a point way down in the foliage, whereas in *L. ×intermedia*, the stems branch above the foliage. Cymes in the flower spike of both species can vary in size and in how close together they are. Fine glandular hairs (woolly indumentum) covering the calyx are more characteristic of *L. angustifolia*, although they are exhibited by some *L. ×intermedia* cultivars, such as 'Gros Bleu'.

INSIDER tip

Which species yields the most oil, *Lavandula angustifolia* or *Lavandula ×intermedia*? Because lavandins are larger plants with bigger flowers, they yield much more essential oil than true lavenders. On average, to extract 1 pound (0.45 kg) of essential oil, 80 pounds (36 kg) of fresh lavandin is needed, compared with 150 pounds (68 kg) of some true lavender cultivars. The difference in output might influence your decision about which species and cultivars to grow.

Characteristic features of *Lavandula angustifolia*.

LAVENDER BASICS

Characteristic features of *Lavandula* ×*intermedia*.

The Pollinator Benefit

The reverberating sounds and waves of movement brought by the bumblebees (*Bombus* species) and honeybees (*Apis mellifera*) in my lavender beds give the impression that plant and insect are one giant organism, with flowers and pollinators working in unison. The flowers provide nectar and pollen, and the bees heartily accept. The scent of lavender's volatile compound linalool, which so appeals to us humans, also appeals to the pollinators.

Lavender produces both nectar and pollen, making a feast for all pollinators. The swirl of movement never ceases to amaze me. My eyes usually spot more bumblebees than honeybees, as the former move more quickly among the flowers. Researchers have found that bumblebees spend from 1.1 to 1.4 seconds per lavender flower, as opposed to the slower honeybees, who spend 3.5 seconds per flower. Researchers have also observed that the bumblebee's longer tongue (or *glossa*) makes it easier to extract the nectar from the lavender flower. In contrast, the honeybee needs to push its head further into the flower to reach the nectar.

If I stand still and watch closely, I can observe many different types of bumblebees in the morning light. As the dawn warms the fields, movement begins to stir. I have unintentionally come across sleeping bees in the golden early light and received an unpleasant surprise. A bottle of lavender essential oil is always in my pocket to soothe stings just in case I make the mistake of not treading carefully when harvesting flowering stems. The oil, especially lavandin essential oil, will take the irritation away and prevent my hand from swelling into a balloon. This is proof that the camphor ketones are actively working.

Studies suggest that lavender is particularly important for bees, as lavender blooms continuously at the peak of summer, when, surprisingly, there is less forage around. This time of year, when early summer blooms have faded and late summer buds are yet to open, is known as the midsummer gap. Certain cultivars of lavender continue to bloom throughout the midsummer gap, and the aromatic flowers provide bees with much-needed nectar.

It is not only chemical compounds like linalool that attract pollinators. So does color, and blue or violet is the top color choice for a bee. The fact is that lavender, blue-flowered borage, and wild marjoram, along with certain clovers, are the flowers most attractive to bees.

A honeybee pollinates a lavender flower.

The Chemistry of Lavender

There is a reason we are attracted to highly aromatic plants. It's all about the chemistry of the plant. What we perceive as fragrance are the plant's aromatic compounds changing state and floating into our noses. When we smell the fragrance of blooming lavender or lavender essential oil, its sweet, herbaceous, and floral notes help us experience a sensation of calm.

Like lavender, many other species of the mint family are loaded with aromatic volatile oils. These rich, spicy aromatic oils make these plants a favorite in cooking. Nearly half the spices in your kitchen come from this one family, including basil, rosemary, lavender, marjoram, thyme, savory, horehound, common sage, and many variations of peppermint and spearmint. You will find similarities among many herbs in the mint family because the chemical constituents are similar, yet each plant has a unique combination of compounds.

The oil glands in lavender flowers produce a complex mixture of more than one hundred phytochemicals. Each of the aromatic compounds contributes to the therapeutic and healing effects we experience when we use essential oils and work with the plant. Essential oils are the superpotent version of a plant. They have the same characteristics as the plant they're derived from, but in a concentrated form.

CAUTION!

Essential oils of some lavender species can be relatively safe to use, while oils from other species should be used only with considerable safety precautions. For instance, oil from spike lavender (*Lavandula latifolia*) has high levels of ketones like camphor and cineole and is not intended for direct use on the body. It is best diluted with a carrier oil, used to scent detergents, or employed as a natural substitute for turpentine, a solvent. Oil from *Lavandula angustifolia* is generally considered safe for use on the body and in perfumes, or with a carrier oil. Some individuals may be more sensitive than others.

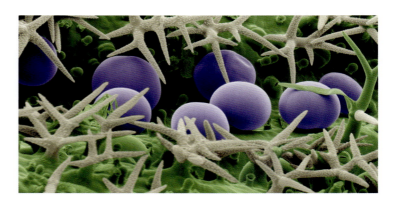

Electron micrograph showing mature essential oil glands (in blue) on the surface of the *Lavandula angustifolia* calyx. The branched pale brown structures are the ribs of the flowers.

Essential oils from different lavender species—and even from different individuals of the same lavender species—can vary greatly in chemical composition, scent, and therapeutic properties. The levels of specific chemical components can differ based on the country and/or region where the plants have grown, the cultivar grown, weather and climate conditions, soil amendments used, how and when flowers are gathered (fully open, partly closed, or at the seed stage) and in which season, how soon the harvest is distilled and how it is distilled (hydro distillation = by steam, versus hydra distillation = in water), and countless other external factors.

Understanding the basic components of lavender's chemistry will give you a foundation to explore and experience the plant at a new level. I highlight the dominant compounds here, but there are many more, and this only scratches the surface.

Terpenes are the aromatic compounds responsible for the scent of most fragrant plants, including members of the mint family. These aromatic oils are volatile and colorless, and they are not soluble in water. You will notice this when you add a drop of lavender essential oil to water, as it will float to the top. A class of terpenes called *monoterpenes* is most recognized when we are discussing the benefits of lavender. Monoterpenes contain powerful antioxidants and are primarily responsible for flavor, aroma, and color in lavender. In particular, the monoterpenes linalyl acetate and linalool confer many of lavender's benefits. Lavender oil may contain up to 40 percent linalyl acetate and 30 percent linalool. Both are nontoxic to humans yet also naturally antimicrobial.

Linalool is one of the dominant compounds in lavender, especially *Lavandula angustifolia*. It belongs to a class of monoterpenes known as alcohols and is responsible for lavender's relaxing aroma and ability to soothe anxious feelings. In topical applications it exhibits antiseptic and repellent activity (making it a great additive to a natural bug spray), cleansing properties (producing an effective household cleaner), and the ability to tonify, balance, and stimulate the skin to heal, keeping skin looking young when added to lotions and toner.

Linalyl acetate, the other dominant compound in lavender, belongs to a class of monoterpenes known as esters. It aids relaxation, acts as an anti-inflammatory, helps soothe muscle spasms, and balances the entire nervous system. The aroma is light and sweet. Linalyl acetate can also calm and uplift one's mood and can induce sleep. Note that although it is not water soluble, trace amounts are still present in lavender hydrosol (the distillate or floral waters the essential oil is siphoned from;

the liquid that comes through the still's condenser). The same is true of linalool, which is considered slightly soluble in water.

Other important monoterpenes in lavender include these:

Cis-beta-ocimene and trans-beta-ocimene, which offer a woodsy and floral scent and have powerful antifungal, antiviral, and anti-inflammatory properties.

Limonene, which is present in the peel and flower of citrus fruits and also found in lesser quantities in lavender, more in lavandins than true lavenders. It works as an expectorant and sedative.

Terpinen-4-ol, which has a pleasant aroma that is well tolerated and is generally used for its antiseptic and pain-relieving properties (physical and emotional).

Borneol, not present in true lavender but commonly present in lavandins, spike lavender, and rosemary. Borneol is known for its minty, earthy, pungent, camphorlike smell. It gives lavender an expectorant property that clears mucus from airways and also has sedative qualities.

Lavandulol, commonly found in trace amounts in lavandins, spike lavender, and true lavender. It smells slightly floral and lemony, with a fruity nuance. Lavandulol and its esters, including *lavandulyl acetate*, are used in the perfume industry and have been identified as insect pheromones.

Ketones, which promote pain relief, relaxation, respiratory health, and cell regeneration. *Camphor* is a distinctive ketone that lends a woodsy, spicy menthol scent commonly compared to eucalyptus and rosemary. It is found in spike lavender and lavandins but usually absent or only slightly present in true lavender.

Phenols, present in higher levels in lavandins than angustifolias. Phenols include *carvacrol* and *thymol*, both known to be antiseptic and antifungal, and *1,8-cineole (eucalyptol)*, which has expectorant properties and is known to repel roaches and scorpions.

The chemistry of lavender leaves and stems is dominated by camphor compounds. Studies show that especially in lavandins, the chemical constituents eucalyptol, camphor and borneol are at their highest levels in the stem and leaf parts of the plant.

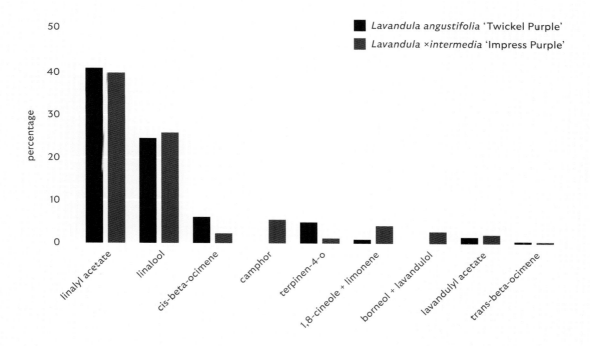

A comparison of the proportions of major compounds present in the steam-distilled essential oil of two different lavender cultivars.

Distilling Essential Oils

I like to distill *Lavandula ×intermedia* (lavandin) and *Lavandula angustifolia* (true lavender) separately in order to take advantage of each plant's chemotype—the unique chemical profile that distinguishes different plants of the same species. The essential oil of *L. ×intermedia* acts as a mild stimulant, with a pungent smell and an invigorating effect. By contrast, the oil of *L. angustifolia* is calming and relaxing, with a sweet and floral scent, due to its particular linalool-to-linalyl-acetate-to-camphor ratio.

My ability to distinguish a lavender's unique volatile compounds is highest at the moment when I am distilling it. By midmorning, I bring freshly harvested flower spikes to the still area and fill what's called a charge, basically a steamer basket, to the brim with fresh lavender. I then fill the pot with water, lower the charge into the pot, and seal the lid tight. I let go of my to-do list and surrender to what the plant has to offer. When the water comes to a boil and the steam begins to penetrate the herb material, I begin to smell the many distinguishing aromas of the desired compounds: floral, sweet, camphor.

Other functional compounds, such as coumarin, aren't detectable to my nose; they require patience and great care to capture. Coumarin, which has been found in 150 plant species, is considered one of the main sedative components of lavender essential oil. I have found that when I am distilling true lavender or lavandin, it is important not to end the distillation prematurely. Coumarin only begins to distill out after eighty to ninety minutes of distillation time.

As a grower and distiller of lavender, I like to be able to judge the quality of the oil I've distilled from a given species and cultivar. I occasionally send a sample to a lab to have a gas chromatography (GC) test done, a technique that can separate and analyze volatile compounds in their gas phase. A GC report shows the quantity of each chemical constituent in a given distillation of lavender essential oil. I can compare my results with the ISO (International Organization for Standardization) standards for lavender essential oils and see if I am in a range that would be considered worthy for medicinal, perfume, and aromatherapy uses.

Acceptability of lavender oil is judged not only through analytical data but also by subjective evaluation or sniff test. People can actually be trained to assess the individual aromatic notes in an essential oil and their overall balance and impact. After many years of distilling, I have begun to associate certain aromas with individual compounds and with individual cultivars. This has helped me in creating signature products and specific applications for each individual essential oil.

clockwise from left

Essential oil floats to the top of the separator and is siphoned off the distillate or what we call hydrosol.

Filling and packing the charge basket with fresh *L. angustifolia* 'Maillette'.

Fresh lavender in the charge basket. The bottle on the left is hydrosol.

Chapter 2

Selecting Your Plants

Choosing lavender for your garden or farm is an exciting endeavor once you know what you would like to achieve. Whether your goal is to incorporate violet hues in your xeriscape garden, create a fragrant border or hedge along a walkway, or start a flower business or lavender farm, you will find many different species and cultivars available to choose from. Each one has unique traits and physical attributes that may make it more desirable than another for your situation.

In this chapter I offer a library of suggestions from the six most common and popular species of lavender. Within each species, I have selected cultivars that are versatile, beautiful, and commonly available, and I detail key attributes of each cultivar. Knowing these details will help you choose the species and cultivars that best suit your circumstances.

Cultivar Attributes

Each plant description in this chapter gives the plant's Latin name and cultivar name plus variations, USDA hardiness zones, origin, habit/size, stem length, spacing, flower color, foliage color, bloom time/frequency, scent, and uses, along with recommended alternatives. Let's walk through these attributes one by one so you can get a clear sense of what to consider when making plant selections.

CULTIVAR NAMES AND VARIATIONS

Often you will find different names given to the same cultivar. This could be due to the particular path the plant took to market, or it could be the name adopted in a specific place in the world. For cultivars that have multiple names, I list alternative designations after the main name. For example, 'Folgate' may also be referred to as 'Folgate Blue'. Additionally, a patented cultivar may carry its patented trade name as well as a cultivar name. For instance, *Lavandula ×intermedia* 'Niko' is sold under the trade name Phenomenal and protected by patent number PP24193.

HARDINESS

A plant's hardiness determines how adaptable it is to colder climates. When thinking about which lavenders will do best where you live, you must consider a plant's hardiness as it relates to your latitude and elevation. Lavender cultivars grow best when planted in zones that match their comfort range. You will find that winter damage occurs most often when plants are out of their hardiness zone. Avoid selecting plants that are only marginally hardy for your region, as this is when you will tend to see winter damage, poor growth, less flowering, and a shortened life span.

The US Department of Agriculture (USDA) offers a plant hardiness zone map online that divides the United States and southern Canada into thirteen different zones, based on average low temperatures in winter, and lets users search for their hardiness zone by zip code. The higher the hardiness zone number, the warmer is the average low temperature in that zone in winter. Choose lavenders rated at your hardiness zone number or lower. For instance, if you live in zone 6a in the United States, don't plant a lavender with a hardiness zone number of 6b or higher. The Royal Horticultural Society (RHS) offers its own simple classification system online, assigning plants to one of four groups based on growing conditions required by the plant to survive rather than geographic locations. The RHS has also developed a system published in the reference work *European Garden Flora* dividing Europe into seven growing zones. Most of the other larger countries and regions of the world also have their own version of a hardiness map, searchable at plantmaps.com.

HARDINESS GROUPS AND LOW TEMPERATURE TOLERANCE RANGES

Hardiness group	Low temperature tolerance range	USDA zones	RHS zones	EGF zones	Lavender species included
Hardy	−20° to 10°F (−29° to −12°C)	4b–9	H5, H6, H7	H2	*L. angustifolia* *L. ×chaytorae*, some cultivars *L. ×intermedia*
Frost-hardy	5° to 30°F (−15° to −1°C)	7–10	H4	H4	*L. ×chaytorae*, most cultivars *L. latifolia* *L. pedunculata* *L. stoechas* *L. viridis*
Half-hardy	25° to 35°F (−4° to 2°C)	9b–12a	H3	H5	*L. dentata* *L. ×heterophylla* *L. lanata*
Tender	32°F (0°C)	10	H2	G1	*L. ×allardii* *L. pterostoechas*

Microclimates always provide exceptions in each hardiness zone. For example, lavender is successfully being grown in microclimates in regions of the Midwest, like Michigan and Wisconsin, and of the South, like Mississippi and Tennessee. Lavender will survive more frost if grown in drier soils than if grown in waterlogged soils. As another example, most of Montana is in USDA zones 3a to 4b, but regions like the Tobacco Valley are in zone 6a. This is considered a "banana belt," a term applied to an area that typically enjoys warmer weather than the surrounding areas, particularly in winter. The banana belt phenomenon occurs in many regions worldwide, including on the lee side of mountain ranges and in areas warmed by adjacent bodies of water. Talk to gardeners and lavender growers in your neighborhood to see which lavenders grow best in your area.

Growing zones are a guide, no more, as climatic conditions are ever changing. What I am accustomed to now is considerably different from when I first started

Lavenders in Four Different Hardiness Groups

Lavenders can be categorized as hardy, frost-hardy, half-hardy, or tender.

HARDY lavenders can generally survive cold temperatures down to –20 degrees F (–29 degrees C).

FROST-HARDY lavenders are hardy in an average winter when the temperature doesn't drop below 5 degrees F (–15 degrees C).

HALF-HARDY lavenders are hardy in a mild winter when temperatures stay above 25 degrees F (–4 degrees C) or when kept in an unheated greenhouse or hoop house.

TENDER lavenders do not tolerate freezes unless they are kept in a frost-free greenhouse.

The hardiest lavenders are the cultivars of *Lavandula angustifolia* and *Lavandula ×intermedia*. These species require a cold period to promote good flowering, so they are not suitable for subtropical and tropical conditions. In the United States, they have proven hardy along the Eastern Seaboard and in the Rocky Mountains, the Pacific Northwest, and the high desert of Utah, New Mexico, and Colorado. Hardy species also include *Lavandula ×chaytorae* (some cultivars, though most are frost-hardy).

Frost-hardy lavenders include *Lavandula stoechas*, and half-hardy lavenders include *Lavandula dentata*.

Tender species, some of the most delicate lavenders, include *Lavandula pterostoechas* and *Lavandula ×allardii*. Flowers of lavender in all three hardiness groups can be enjoyed year-round if the plants are grown in pots and moved indoors for winter. They make a delightful display outside from May to October but need to be brought inside before the first frost and kept warm at around 40 degrees F (5 degrees C) or above in a greenhouse, hoop house, garage, or home. Alternatively, they can be treated as annuals if you plant them in spring and enjoy them for one growing season, or they can be grown outdoors in USDA zones 10a and above year-round.

Tender species can withstand high humidity, but extended periods of high humidity are difficult for hardy and frost-hardy cultivars. Similarly, there is an upper limit on the temperatures the various groups of lavenders can take.

The table shows the hardiness groups, their low temperature tolerance range on average, and their zones according to three different classification systems: USDA, RHS, and European Garden Flora (EGF). The tolerance range is meant to suggest that not all cultivars in a particular group can withstand the lowest temperature, especially for a long period of time, but all can withstand the highest low temperature in the range.

growing lavender. Weather patterns are more erratic. The last hard freeze dates have been unpredictable. The first hard frost of the season in my growing zone and at my elevation was typically in the late fall, but now it may occur before plants have entered dormancy, meaning many of my perennials are at risk of tissue damage or plant death. Plant selection and growing methods need to be flexible and inventive. For example, I may have floating blanket covers handy for unexpected cold snaps or choose lavender cultivars that withstand extreme temperatures, both hot and cold, more readily. Finding methods to trick plants to enter dormancy sooner or delay pruning until spring are just a few ideas to consider.

Additionally, it is not just cold hardiness and temperature that will affect your success, it is also the duration and intensity of the light the plants receive throughout the year. Lavender needs a minimum of six hours of full sun per day. Full sun is not the same as you move farther north or south of the equator, dictating that lavender is best grown between the 48th parallel north and the 20th parallel south. Successful growing south of the 33rd parallel will depend on the specific growing conditions of a given region or microclimate.

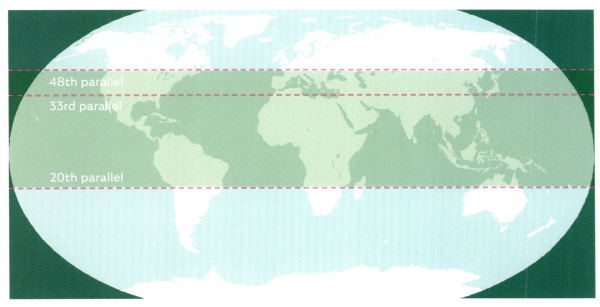

Latitudes where lavender grows best: between the 48th parallel north (top) and the 20th parallel south (bottom).

SELECTING YOUR PLANTS 39

ORIGIN

Lavender cultivars have a rich history. Some lavender cultivars popular today date back as far as the nineteenth century. Each entry here tells who developed the plant, where, and the year it was introduced to the public. Understanding a plant's origin can lend some insight into how well it fits your needs and desires. For example, some species and cultivars were developed for their high-quality oil, their deep purple color, or their striking landscape qualities. In the most comprehensive account of lavender published to date, *The Genus Lavandula*, authors Tim Upson and Susyn Andrews have done an amazing job of compiling the history and cultivation of thirty-nine species, their hybrids, and at least four hundred cultivars. Some of the origin stories I have included are based on their research.

HABIT AND SIZE

Habit is the shape and form in summer when the plant is in full bloom. The shape can be splayed, bushy, or upright, depending on the lavender species and cultivar. The form can be tight and compact or loose and spreading.

Size is the average height and width when the plant is fully flowering. Lavender is considered full grown by year three but continues to grow until year five. Generally, lavenders grow as wide as they are tall. A plant can be as narrow as 18 inches (45 cm) or as wide as 52 inches (132 cm), depending on the species, the cultivar, and the growing conditions.

STEM LENGTH

Stem length is the average length of the main stem or peduncle, including the primary spike or flower. Some lavender stems are branched and some are unbranched. The primary stem can vary from 3 to 30 inches long. Branched stems have laterals varying from 4 to 10 inches long. Stem length is affected not only by species and cultivar but also by growing conditions and climate.

SPACING

Spacing is the recommended distance from neighboring plants in order to grow a healthy plant with adequate space to bloom. It is based on how large the fully grown plant is expected to be in five years, with the understanding that the growth rate can be affected by zone, climate, and soil type. I suggest a range of spacings, with the lower end giving a tighter effect, more like a hedgerow.

FLOWER COLOR

Lavender flowers aren't just blue or purple. Some lavenders can bloom a subtle light purple or a dark, rich Mediterranean blue. Others have blush pink, pure white, or silver-gray flowers.

When we talk about the flowers of a lavender plant, it's the corolla (petals) of lavender species like *Lavandula angustifolia* and *L. ×intermedia* we are referring to, not the calyx (sepals). The calyx color does vary from the corolla color; many times, it can be darker than the corolla. In essence, you get to enjoy two different colors in the growing season: the calyx color when the buds are closed and the corolla color when the flowers are fully open. For lavender species *L. stoechas* and *L. dentata*, the apical bracts are the colored parts.

Color designations can vary widely since the perception of color and its naming depend on the observer. To uniformly describe color throughout this book, I will refer to corolla color only and use the nomenclature of the Royal Horticultural Society (RHS) Colour Chart, the standard reference used by horticulturists worldwide for identifying plant colors. In cards resembling paint samples, the most recent version of the chart (sixth edition, 2015) shows 920 colors that can be matched precisely to flowers, fruits, and other plant parts in order to record and communicate colors accurately across the world. Distinct colors are given a number and a letter—for example, bright violet-blue is RHS 90B. The plant entries in this chapter give a description of the flower color as well as the RHS color number and letter.

In the bloom color and uses tables later in this section, as well as in the plant entries for *L. angustifolia* and *L. ×intermedia*, cultivars are grouped by the color of their blooms to help you select the best cultivars for your purposes.

VIOLET FLOWERS: This group includes plants with flower colors varying from dark violet (RHS 83A) to vibrant soft violet (RHS 88D).

VIOLET-BLUE FLOWERS: This group includes plants with flowers in shades of dark violet-blue (RHS 90A), bright violet-blue (RHS 90B), and violet-blue (RHS 90C).

LAVENDER TO MID VIOLET FLOWERS: This group includes plants with flower colors such as mid violet (RHS 86B) and soft lavender-violet (RHS 92A).

PINK FLOWERS: This group includes plants with flowers in shades including off pink (RHS 69B) and mid pink mauve (RHS 75A).

If you are selling fresh-cut flower bouquets or dried lavender bundles, your clientele may have color preferences. Historically, in the United States consumers prefer the darkest of violets, while in France they prefer light violet colors, and in the UK, blue hues are preferred. Another influence on color selection is the sensation you want to feel when you walk into your garden or down a pathway. Blue hues project calm, while dark purple tones project royalty and strength.

This lavender flower has bright violet-blue (RHS 90B) petals and a much lighter calyx.

Colors of Fresh and Dried Lavenders, Compared

Over time, the color of a lavender's flowers can change and fade. Some cultivars hold on longer than others to their first bloom colors. If the stems are cut and dried, the colors change from what they were in their fresh form. Lavenders vary in how vibrant their colors can be when dried. If you are interested in dried flowers, this may influence your selection of which cultivars to grow. The images here compare the colors of fresh-cut and dried lavenders of the two most popular species.

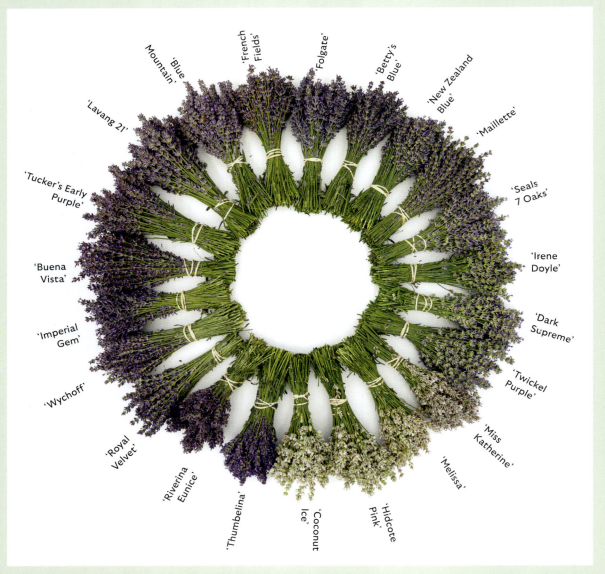

Bundles of fresh-cut *Lavandula angustifolia* organized by color grouping.

44 LAVENDER FOR ALL SEASONS

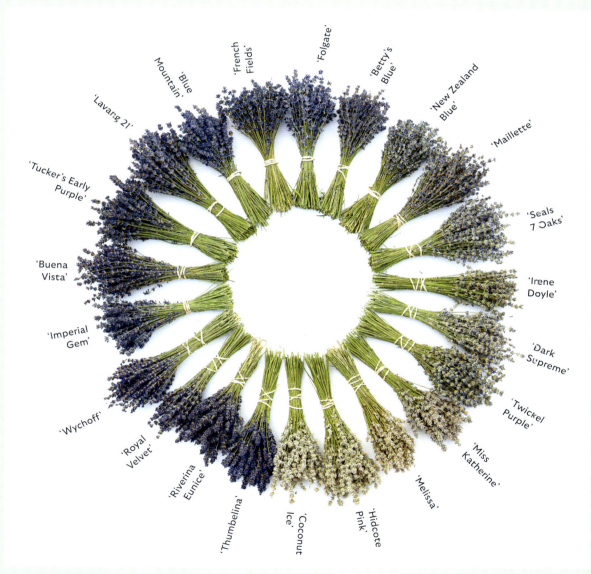

Bundles of dried *Lavandula angustifolia* organized by color grouping.

SELECTING YOUR PLANTS 45

Colors of Fresh and Dried Lavenders, Compared

Bundles of fresh-cut *Lavandula* ×*intermedia* organized by color grouping.

Bundles of dried *Lavandula* ×*intermedia* organized by color grouping.

FOLIAGE COLOR

Leaves can vary from light green to silver. The foliage color given for each cultivar is during the summer months and is described as light green, mid green, gray-green, or gray. During winter, or when the plants are dormant, leaf color is gray, especially in *L. angustifolia* species, and silver to gray in *L. ×intermedia* species.

BLOOM TIMING AND FREQUENCY

One beauty of lavender is that you can choose varieties for your garden that bloom at different times, providing you with color throughout spring, summer, and fall. Some lavenders bloom only once, some bloom multiple times during the growing season, and some bloom continually as long as you are harvesting or deadheading the flowers, removing both flower and stem once the blooms are spent or have gone to seed. Bloom frequency is mainly dictated by species, cultivar, length of your growing season, and how soon flowers are harvested.

In my garden there is only a four-week period during spring and summer when I don't have any blooms. I extend the blooms by growing three different species and a variety of cultivars within those species. In considering when and how often lavender might bloom in your garden, your first step is identifying your USDA zone, altitude, and latitude. As an example, if you live in USDA zone 4b or 5a at 7000 feet and the 37th parallel north, you may be limited to growing only *Lavandula angustifolia*. Even within that species, your bloom time will vary compared to a garden located at 680 feet in USDA zone 10a at the 33rd parallel north.

Our farm in Colorado is in USDA zone 7a at 4800 feet and the 39th parallel north, but the growing conditions and weather make it closer to zone 5b or 6. Our lavender bloom begins in mid-June and goes through mid-November. For me to grow *L. stoechas* or have blooming lavender in pots in the month of May, I maintain the plants in a hoop house and greenhouses in the winter and early spring months. In mid-June, our early-blooming true lavenders—*L. angustifolia* 'Folgate', 'Croxton's Wild', and 'Miss Katherine'—start blooming. As our season progresses, 'Buena Vista' and 'Royal Velvet' reach full bloom by late June. At the beginning of July, our *L. ×intermedia* cultivars begin to show a hue of color through their calyx, and they start to reach full bloom by mid-July, beginning with 'Riverina Thomas' and then 'Impress Purple'.

Extending Your Bloom with Different Cultivars

You can extend your bloom by incorporating different lavender species and cultivars in your garden. The tables here for *L. angustifolia* and *L. ×intermedia* will give you an idea how.

Full bloom is defined as the period when at least 50 percent of the calyx or flower buds are open. Full bloom typically lasts three to four weeks, depending on when and if you decide to harvest your flowers. Frequency of bloom means how many times a particular cultivar can be expected to bloom throughout the growing season. Some lavenders, which I call double bloomers, bloom twice with the same extent of flowers each time. Others, which I call continuous bloomers, have one abundant bloom and then once the flowers have been harvested or deadheaded, have a covering of blooms throughout the season.

The timing of seasons shown in the tables is based on your USDA zone. For example, in zone 5a and 5b in the United States, late spring and early summer extend until June 20; midsummer spans from the end of June through July; late summer begins in August and goes through mid-September; fall reaches from mid-September through November, and the first hard frost may arrive by mid-November. In the Southern Hemisphere, bloom time in similar climates would be mid-December through January and can be as late as mid-February.

BLOOM COLOR, FREQUENCY, AND TIMING FOR POPULAR *LAVANDULA ANGUSTIFOLIA* CULTIVARS

● indicates full bloom time during the flowering season.

	RHS color of corolla	Bloom frequency	Blooms late spring to early summer	Blooms midsummer	Blooms late summer	Blooms fall
VIOLET FLOWERS						
'Betty's Blue'	mid violet, 86C	one full bloom to continuous bloom		●		
'Croxton's Wild'	vibrant violet, 88A	one full bloom	●			
'Folgate'	dark violet, 83A	one full bloom to continuous bloom	●			
'Irene Doyle'	vibrant violet, 88A	double bloom	●			●
'Lavang 21'	vibrant violet, 88A	double bloom	●			●
'Purple Bouquet'	vibrant violet, 88A	double bloom			●	●

	RHS color of corolla	Bloom frequency	Blooms late spring to early summer	Blooms midsummer	Blooms late summer	Blooms fall
VIOLET-BLUE FLOWERS						
'Buena Vista'	bright violet-blue, 90B	multiple bloom	●		●	●
'Imperial Gem'	bright violet-blue, 90B	double bloom	●			●
'Maillette'	dark violet-blue, 90A	one full bloom minimum		●	●	
'Melissa Lilac'	violet-blue, 90C	one full bloom	●	●		
'Pacific Blue'	dark violet-blue, 90A	double bloom		●		●
'Royal Velvet'	violet-blue, 90C	double bloom		●		●
'Sharon Roberts'	bright violet-blue, 90B	double bloom		●		●
'SuperBlue'	dark violet-blue, 90A	one full bloom to continuous bloom		●		
'Thumbelina Leigh'	dark lavender-violet, 94A	double bloom		●		●
'Tucker's Early Purple'	dark violet-blue, 90A	double bloom	●			●
LAVENDER TO MID VIOLET FLOWERS						
'Dark Supreme'	violet to violet-blue, 88A to 89A	double bloom	●			●
'French Fields'	mid lavender-violet, 92A	double bloom		●		
'True Munstead'	mid violet, 86B	double bloom	●			●
PINK FLOWERS						
'Coconut Ice'	mid pink mauve, 75A	one full bloom	●			
'Hidcote Pink'	opening off pink, 69B, to pale mauve pink, 76C; maturing to mid pink mauve, 77C	one full bloom	●			
'Melissa'	opening white; maturing to off pink, 69B, to soft pink mauve in the center, 75B	one full bloom	●			
'Miss Katherine'	mid pink mauve, 75A, to off gray-pink, 69D	one full bloom	●			
WHITE						
'Nana Alba'	white	one full bloom	●			

SELECTING YOUR PLANTS

BLOOM COLOR, FREQUENCY, AND TIMING FOR POPULAR
LAVANDULA ×INTERMEDIA CULTIVARS

● indicates full bloom time during the flowering season.

	RHS color of corolla	Bloom frequency	Blooms late spring to early summer	Blooms midsummer	Blooms late summer	Blooms fall
VIOLET FLOWERS						
'Gros Bleu'	dark violet, 83A	one full bloom		●	●	
'Grosso'	vibrant violet, 88A, to soft violet, 86A	one full bloom		●	●	
'Impress Purple'	vibrant violet, 88A	one full bloom		●		●
VIOLET-BLUE FLOWERS						
'Hidcote Giant'	bright violet-blue, 90B	one full bloom		●		
'Niko'	violet-blue, 90D	one full bloom	●	●		
'Provence'	lavender-violet, 94C	one full bloom to continous bloom		●	●	●
'Riverina Thomas'	bright violet-blue, 90B	one full bloom to continuous bloom		●		●
'Seal'	violet-blue, 90C	one full bloom		●	●	
'Super'	violet-blue, 90C	one full bloom			●	
WHITE FLOWERS						
'Edelweiss'	white	one full bloom			●	

SCENT

Scent is the general aroma profile of a particular cultivar. For example, notes of sweet, floral, clove, herbal, camphor, or mint commonly best describe the smell of lavender flowers, although how scents are described can vary according to people's perceptions. Scent can also vary with climate and growing conditions. Still, some cultivars do have distinct aromas compared to others due to their specific chemical makeup. A lavandin contains a higher proportion of camphor compounds than true lavender and therefore gives off more of a eucalyptus or menthol note. Conversely, true lavender, with higher levels of linalool compounds, produces sweet, floral notes.

USES

After many years of growing, handling, and processing different lavender cultivars, I have learned which qualities make one cultivar more useful than another for a specific purpose or need. For instance, some cultivars yield high amounts of quality essential oil, while others maintain color and hold on to buds tightly when dried and therefore make the best wreaths and bouquets. While all lavenders are useful in landscapes, some lavenders are so compact as to create a wonderful hedge along a walkway, while others are so large they make a striking focal point in a garden bed. Specific cultivars of *Lavandula angustifolia* are exceptional for lending a fresh mint or spice note to a simple syrup or an herbal beverage infusion. Each plant description in this chapter shows the best uses for that cultivar.

ALTERNATIVES

Availability of plants can vary greatly depending on where you are in the world. The closer you live to lavender farms or lavender growing regions, the more likely it is that small boutique nurseries in your area will carry multiple species and cultivars. These nurseries are often very specialized and may focus on lavender and other herbs. You will find the patented and most common lavender cultivars in neighborhood nurseries and large garden centers. Online you can find quite a lavender selection and many nurseries that will ship individual plants. The Resources section of this book lists a few nurseries that do ship. But if you find it hard to obtain a cultivar described in the entries that follow, you may be able to find one of the alternatives I recommend, cultivars with similar attributes such as color, form, or use.

Best Lavenders for Various Uses

The following tables give a quick overview of which cultivars are best for which uses.

BEST USES OF POPULAR *LAVANDULA ANGUSTIFOLIA* CULTIVARS

	🌳	🪴	🏺	🌾	✂️	🥣	💧	🧴
VIOLET FLOWERS								
'Betty's Blue'	●			●	●	●		
'Croxton's Wild'	●					●		
'Folgate'	●		●	●		●		
'Irene Doyle'	●						●	●
'Lavang 21'	●			●	●	●		
'Purple Bouquet'	●			●	●			
VIOLET-BLUE FLOWERS								
'Buena Vista'	●			●	●	●		●
'Imperial Gem'	●	●				●		●
'Maillette'	●						●	●
'Melissa Lilac'	●		●			●		
'Pacific Blue'	●		●	●		●		●
'Royal Velvet'	●		●	●		●		●
'Sharon Roberts'	●			●	●	●		
'SuperBlue'	●	●	●	●		●	●	●
'Thumbelina Leigh'	●	●			●			
'Tucker's Early Purple'	●					●		
LAVENDER TO MID VIOLET FLOWERS								
'Dark Supreme'	●			●	●	●		
'French Fields'	●			●		●	●	
'True Munstead'	●				●	●		
PINK FLOWERS								
'Coconut Ice'	●	●						
'Hidcote Pink'	●					●	●	●
'Melissa'	●	●				●		
'Miss Katherine'	●			●	●	●	●	●
WHITE FLOWERS								
'Nana Alba'	●	●				●	●	●

LAVENDER FOR ALL SEASONS

BEST USES OF POPULAR *LAVANDULA ×INTERMEDIA* CULTIVARS

	Landscape	Container	Fresh-cut	Dried	Crafting	Culinary	Essential oil	Hydrosol
VIOLET FLOWERS								
'Gros Bleu'	●		●		●	●		
'Grosso'	●		●		●		●	●
'Impress Purple'	●		●	●	●		●	●
VIOLET-BLUE FLOWERS								
'Hidcote Giant'	●		●	●	●			
'Niko'	●		●	●				
'Provence'	●		●		●	●		
'Riverina Thomas'	●		●	●	●		●	●
'Seal'	●		●		●		●	●
'Super'	●		●	●			●	●
WHITE FLOWERS								
'Edelweiss'	●		●	●	●		●	●

KEY:

Landscape. All lavenders are useful in landscapes, though how they can be incorporated varies widely.

Container. Lavenders for containers are generally compact, have tight mounds and shorter stems, and do not get very large.

Fresh-cut bundle. Lavenders can make beautiful fresh-cut bundles due to their stem length, color, and long-lasting bloom that ensures their color will be maintained after being picked.

Dried bundle. Lavenders that dry well for wreaths and bouquets tend to shatter less (keep their buds), maintain their color, and have long stems.

Crafting buds. Some lavenders produce aromatic buds that clean easily and make a colorful potpourri.

Culinary. Lavenders suitable for culinary creations have a flavor profile that enhances savory or sweet dishes.

Essential oil. Some lavenders give a high yield and/or produce a high quality of essential oil.

Hydrosol. When lavender flowers are steam- or hydra-distilled, they produce a distillate or hydrosol with healing properties.

SELECTING YOUR PLANTS 53

Lavandula angustifolia

Lavandula angustifolia, also called true lavender or common lavender, is the most widely grown lavender species around the world. In French the common name is *lavande* or *lavande vraie*, in Spanish *lavanda fina*, and in Italian *lavanda*. It is the most cold-hardy species and flourishes in various climates; in fact, every one of the cultivars listed here can be grown at higher elevations and has been proven to withstand cold temperatures.

This species is best known and prized for its essential oils, its use as a landscape or herb-garden plant, and its culinary use in sweet and savory dishes. It offers a wide variety of colors, shapes, and sizes. Though most of the lavender cultivars listed here were introduced in the nineteenth and twentieth centuries, their genetic lines go back hundreds of years.

Lavandula angustifolia blooms earlier than *Lavandula ×intermedia* cultivars, at the end of spring and beginning of summer. If pruned lightly or immediately after the first harvest, some cultivars will bloom throughout summer and again in fall.

'Hidcote' and 'Vera' are absent from the plant entries. True 'Hidcote' is rare and difficult to find (as is true 'Munstead', which I did include), especially in the United States. These commonly used names refer to plants that are grown from seed and can vary considerably, losing many of the original traits, so the color and plant size vary from the parent plant. 'Hidcote', 'Vera', and 'Munstead' offered in large nurseries are more likely than not seed-grown, and according to the botanist Dr. Arthur Tucker, these cultivars should be referred to as 'Compacta'—a catchall name for seed-grown varieties.

VIOLET FLOWERS

● *Lavandula angustifolia* 'Betty's Blue'

In our gardens in the high desert of Colorado, 'Betty's Blue' is one of the hardiest and has lasted the longest of the true lavenders.

HARDINESS: USDA zones 5–9; tolerates heat and humidity

ORIGIN: introduced by Nichols Garden Nursery in Albany, Oregon, in 1998; named after Betty Walker, the propagator and manager there

HABIT, HEIGHT × WIDTH: compact mound, 24 × 30 inches (60 × 76 cm)

STEM LENGTH: 10–12 inches (25–30 cm)

SPACING: 24–36 inches (60–90 cm)

FLOWER COLOR: mid violet, RHS 86C

FOLIAGE COLOR: mid green

BLOOMS: blooms midsummer, then continuous bloom after flowers are harvested

SCENT: mild, sweetly floral

USES: landscape, fresh-cut and dried bundles, crafting (retains color and buds when harvested, great for wreaths and dried floral arrangements), culinary, essential oil

ALTERNATIVES: 'SuperBlue'

SELECTING YOUR PLANTS

● ● *Lavandula angustifolia* 'Croxton's Wild'

In our gardens, this cultivar is the first to bloom along with 'Folgate', making it a delightful gift to pollinators after a cold, early spring. With its prolific blooms, it's a great addition to the beekeeper's garden and a must for tea blends.

HARDINESS: USDA zones 5–9

ORIGIN: introduced by Thomas DeBaggio, Arlington, Virginia, in 1994; named after Pauline Croxton of Placerville, California, a commercial grower of tender lavenders who provided DeBaggio with seed that she gathered from wild European populations

HABIT, HEIGHT × WIDTH: well shaped with robust bloom and vigorous growth, 24 × 42 inches (60 × 107 cm)

STEM LENGTH: 7–10 inches (18–25 cm)

SPACING: 36–42 inches (90–107 cm)

FLOWER COLOR: vibrant violet to bright violet-blue, RHS 88A to 90B; blossoms appear white before opening

FOLIAGE COLOR: gray-green

BLOOMS: once early in spring, even in colder zones

SCENT: sweet

USES: landscape, culinary

ALTERNATIVES: 'Dark Supreme', 'Irene Doyle'

● *Lavandula angustifolia* 'Folgate'

Also known as 'Folgate Blue', 'Folgate Dwarf', 'Folgate Variety'

On our farm, 'Folgate' is the first to bloom each season. Cutting bundles of 'Folgate' as the sun comes up, surrounded by the smell of ripe sweet cherries being harvested, inspired me to make lavender cherry jam.

HARDINESS: USDA zones 4b–9

ORIGIN: from Folgate Nursery in Heacham, Norfolk, owned by the Chilvers family, who named it 'Folgate Blue'; believed to have come into being before 1933; won the prestigious award of garden merit from the Royal Horticultural Society in 2012

HABIT, HEIGHT × WIDTH: compact and spreading, 30 × 36 inches (75 × 90 cm)

STEM LENGTH: 12 inches (30 cm)

SPACING: 30–36 inches apart (76–90 cm)

FLOWER COLOR: dark violet, RHS 83A

FOLIAGE COLOR: gray-green

BLOOMS: full bloom late spring/early summer, then continuous bloom after flowers are picked

SCENT: mild mint note, slightly floral

USES: landscape, fresh-cut and dried bundles, culinary (lends itself well to jams from all types of stone fruit, including peaches, cherries, and apricots)

ALTERNATIVES: 'Betty's Blue', 'New Zealand Blue', 'SuperBlue'

SELECTING YOUR PLANTS

●● *Lavandula angustifolia* 'Irene Doyle'

Also known as 'Two Seasons'

HARDINESS: USDA zones 5–9

ORIGIN: selected from mass commercial seed and developed by Thomas DeBaggio, who named it after his mother-in-law, Irene Doyle; introduced in 1981

HABIT, HEIGHT × WIDTH: small to medium, tight and erect plant with vigorous growth, 30 × 30 inches (75 × 76 cm)

STEM LENGTH: 8–10 inches (20–25 cm)

SPACING: 30–36 inches (76–90 cm)

FLOWER COLOR: vibrant violet to bright violet-blue, RHS 88A to 90B; when beginning to flower, calyxes or flower buds show white

FOLIAGE COLOR: gray-green

BLOOMS: late spring/early summer and again in fall, hence its alternative name, 'Two Seasons'

SCENT: very fragrant

USES: landscape, essential oil (excellent production in both quality and quantity), hydrosol

ALTERNATIVES: 'Maillette', 'Dark Supreme'

● *Lavandula angustifolia* 'Lavang 21'

Also marketed under the trade name Violet Intrigue (PP15344)

HARDINESS: USDA zones 5–9

ORIGIN: raised by Virginia McNaughton and Dennis Matthews in 1995 and introduced in 2002 in New Zealand; part of the Twickel group of longer-stemmed plants that also includes 'Royal Velvet', 'Royal Purple'

HABIT, HEIGHT × WIDTH: upright, with spikes evenly distributed, 30 × 36 inches (75 × 90 cm)

STEM LENGTH: 12–14 inches (30–36 cm)

SPACING: 30–36 inches (76–90 cm)

FLOWER COLOR: vibrant violet, RHS 88A

FOLIAGE COLOR: gray-green

BLOOMS: twice, mid-June to early July, fall

SCENT: fragrant, sweet

USES: landscape (in mass or large groupings), fresh-cut and dried bundles, culinary

ALTERNATIVES: 'Royal Velvet', 'Wyckoff'

● *Lavandula angustifolia* 'Purple Bouquet'

HARDINESS: USDA zones 5–9

ORIGIN: developed and introduced at Sunshine Herb Farm, Tenino, Washington, in 2006

HABIT, HEIGHT × WIDTH: splayed, with long stems, 30 × 36 inches (75 × 90 cm)

STEM LENGTH: 12–14 inches (30–36 cm)

SPACING: 30–36 inches (76–90 cm)

FLOWER COLOR: vibrant violet, RHS 88A

FOLIAGE COLOR: gray-green

BLOOMS: twice, midsummer and early fall

SCENT: sweet and spicy

USES: landscape, fresh-cut and dried flower bouquets

ALTERNATIVES: 'Sharon Roberts', 'Buena Vista', 'Fiona English'

VIOLET-BLUE FLOWERS

● *Lavandula angustifolia* 'Buena Vista'

Stems of this cultivar have spaces between the calyxes, making them shatter more easily than lavenders with tightly formed corollas along their stems, such as 'Royal Velvet' or 'Betty's Blue'. It has thin and branchy stems, so if you propagate from cuttings, make long cuttings that include three to five leaf nodes; I suggest cutting just above the last two or three nodes.

HARDINESS: USDA zones 5–9

ORIGIN: raised by Dr. Don Roberts of Premier Botanicals Ltd., Albany, Oregon, for more than five years before releasing in 1988

HABIT, HEIGHT × WIDTH: medium splayed shrub with long interrupted spikes, 30 × 36 inches (75 × 90 cm)

STEM LENGTH: 12–14 inches (30–36 cm)

SPACING: 30–36 inches (76–90 cm)

FLOWER COLOR: bright violet-blue, RHS 90B

FOLIAGE COLOR: light green

BLOOMS: early summer, late summer, and fall, multiple times if flowers are harvested or removed after initial bloom; as many as four blooms under ideal conditions

SCENT: very fragrant and sweet

USES: landscape (hedging), fresh-cut and dried bundles, culinary, essential oil (high quality but quite low yields)

ALTERNATIVES: 'Purple Bouquet', 'Sharon Roberts'

SELECTING YOUR PLANTS

🟣 *Lavandula angustifolia* 'Imperial Gem'

Also known as 'Nana 1'

HARDINESS: USDA zones 5–9

ORIGIN: selected in the 1960s by Norfolk Lavender from a batch of seed planted in search of a new cultivar for their field trials; originally known as 'Nana 1' but changed to 'Imperial Gem' by Henry Head in the mid-1980s; awarded an Award of Garden Merit in 2002

HABIT, HEIGHT × WIDTH: Compact, bushy, and medium size, slightly splayed, 24 × 24 inches (60 × 60 cm)

STEM LENGTH: 10–14 inches (25–36 cm)

SPACING: 24–30 inches (60–76 cm)

FLOWER COLOR: mid lavender-violet, RHS 92A

FOLIAGE COLOR: gray-green

BLOOMS: twice, spring and fall

SCENT: sweet and strong

USES: landscape (edging), container, culinary, hydrosol

ALTERNATIVES: 'Hidcote A', 'Gray Lady'; 'Imperial Gem' is like a true strain of 'Hidcote' but with larger flowers and longer stems

●● *Lavandula angustifolia* 'Maillette'

Also known as 'Mailette'

'Maillette' (pronounced "may-ette") is the main field variety grown in France. It is grown for its essential oil for the perfume industry, producing an oil with a vibrant floral quality that comes from consistently high levels of linalool and linalyl acetate. Sensitive to wind, so the first two to three years, I cover and create a wind block to get the plants established. Responds well to spring pruning.

HARDINESS: USDA zones 5–9; very hardy when established

ORIGIN: perhaps introduced by Pierre Grosso, or by Monsieur Maillet from Valensole, France; widely planted in the 1950s and continues to be a mainstay for essential oil production

HABIT, HEIGHT × WIDTH: medium to large bushy plant, 30 × 42 inches (75 × 107 cm)

STEM LENGTH: 12–14 inches (30–36 cm)

SPACING: 36–42 inches (90–107 cm)

FLOWER COLOR: dark violet-blue, RHS 90A, paling to violet-blue, RHS 90D; can be violet-blue or paling to white in the center of the corolla

FOLIAGE COLOR: mid green

BLOOMS: once in midsummer, holding bloom for four weeks; may rebloom some seasons

SCENT: fresh and floral, strongly fragrant

USES: landscape, essential oil (high yield with steam distillation), hydrosol

ALTERNATIVES: 'Irene Doyle'

SELECTING YOUR PLANTS

● *Lavandula angustifolia* 'Melissa Lilac'

Also known as 'Dow4' and sold under the trade name Melissa Lilac (EU PVR EU21995)

This cultivar has a sport (a genetic mutation that naturally occurs) named 'Opal Rain' with powdery pink flowers and a softly sweet fragrance that has become popular for culinary purposes.

HARDINESS: USDA zones 5–9; excellent winter hardiness and also tolerates heat and humidity

ORIGIN: developer unknown; introduced to market by Downderry Nursery in Kent, UK, in 2003

HABIT, HEIGHT × WIDTH: compact mound, upright, 24 × 30 inches (60 × 76 cm)

STEM LENGTH: 12–14 inches (30–36 cm)

SPACING: 30 inches (76 cm)

FLOWER COLOR: violet-blue, RHS 90C, with light white center and fuzzy violet calyx

FOLIAGE COLOR: gray-green

BLOOMS: once, early to mid summer

SCENT: mildly sweet, musk tones

USES: landscape (borders), fresh-cut bundles, culinary

● *Lavandula angustifolia* 'Pacific Blue'

Also known as '565/6'

HARDINESS: USDA zones 5–9

ORIGIN: imported from France to New Zealand and named by Peter Smale, formerly of the Redbank Research Center, in the early 1990s; developed to be used for essential oil and the fresh-cut flower trade

HABIT, HEIGHT × WIDTH: compact mound, 24 × 24 inches (60 × 60 cm)

STEM LENGTH: 10–12 inches (25–30 cm)

SPACING: 24–30 inches (60–76 cm)

FLOWER COLOR: dark violet-blue, RHS 90A

FOLIAGE COLOR: mid green

BLOOMS: double bloom, midsummer and fall, then continuous bloom after flowers are harvested

SCENT: fresh, peppery and fragrant

USES: landscape (hedging), fresh-cut and dried bundles (retains color and buds when harvested), culinary, essential oil, hydrosol

ALTERNATIVES: 'Betty's Blue', 'Armtipp01' (trade name Big Time Blue, PP24827)

SELECTING YOUR PLANTS   67

● *Lavandula angustifolia* 'Royal Velvet'

HARDINESS: USDA zones 5–9

ORIGIN: raised by Andrew Van Hevelingen of Van Hevelingen Herb Nursery, Newburg, Oregon, and introduced in 1988

HABIT, HEIGHT × WIDTH: compact mound with long stems, 24 × 30 inches (60 × 76 cm)

STEM LENGTH: 12–14 inches (30–36 cm)

SPACING: 30–36 inches (76–90 cm)

FLOWER COLOR: violet-blue, RHS 90C

FOLIAGE COLOR: gray-green

BLOOMS: midsummer and fall

SCENT: very fragrant and sweet

USES: landscape, fresh-cut flowers, dried flower bundles, arrangements, culinary

ALTERNATIVES: 'Lavang 21', 'Wyckoff'

● *Lavandula angustifolia* 'Sharon Roberts'

HARDINESS: USDA zones 5–9

ORIGIN: introduced in 1989 by Don Roberts of Albany, Oregon

HABIT, HEIGHT × WIDTH: splayed growth with long stems, 24 × 30 inches (60 × 76 cm)

STEM LENGTH: 12–16 inches (30–40 cm)

SPACING: 30–36 inches (76–90 cm)

FLOWER COLOR: bright violet-blue, RHS 90B, paler in the center appearing mid violet mauve

FOLIAGE COLOR: gray-green

BLOOMS: twice, summer and fall

SCENT: sweet

USES: landscape, fresh-cut and dried bundles, culinary

ALTERNATIVES: similar to 'Buena Vista' in its bloom, but overall larger in shrub size and stem length; like 'Purple Bouquet', considered part of the Twickel Group (exceptionally long stems)

SELECTING YOUR PLANTS

● *Lavandula angustifolia* 'Thumbelina Leigh'

Also known by its plant patent number, PP15231

Stunning when in bloom. Its compact size makes this cultivar well suited for raised beds or as an edging to a flower bed.

HARDINESS: USDA zones 5–9

ORIGIN: dwarf selection raised by Elsie and Brian Hall, North Island, New Zealand, in the mid-1990s

HABIT, HEIGHT × WIDTH: small, compact, and spherical, 12 × 20 inches (30 × 51 cm)

STEM LENGTH: 3–6 inches (8–15 cm)

SPACING: 18–24 inches (45–60 cm)

FLOWER COLOR: dark lavender-violet, RHS 94A

FOLIAGE COLOR: mid green

BLOOMS: twice, sometimes more when flowers are cut

SCENT: sweet

USES: landscape (edging, raised beds, rock gardens) container, crafting with small stems

ALTERNATIVES: 'Lavenite Petite', 'Imperial Gem', 'Lady' (historically grown from seed), 'Wee One'

● *Lavandula angustifolia* 'Tucker's Early Purple'

HARDINESS: USDA zones 5–9

ORIGIN: developed and introduced by Thomas DeBaggio in 1993 in Arlington, Virginia; said to be a cross between 'Mitcham Grey' and 'Irene Doyle'

HABIT, HEIGHT × WIDTH: compact, medium-size bushy plant, 30 × 30 inches (75 × 76 cm)

STEM LENGTH: 10–12 inches (25–30 cm)

SPACING: 30–36 inches (76–90 cm)

FLOWER COLOR: dark violet-blue, RHS 90A

FOLIAGE COLOR: gray-green

BLOOMS: first to bloom in spring, long lasting and will bloom in fall if summer flowers are harvested or removed

SCENT: sweet

USES: landscape (hedging, grown in a mass or as a single specimen), essential oil

ALTERNATIVES: 'Blue Mountain', 'Hidcote Superior', 'Riverina Eunice'

LAVENDER FOR ALL SEASONS

LAVENDER TO MID VIOLET FLOWERS

●● *Lavandula angustifolia* 'Dark Supreme'

Also known as 'W. K. Doyle', 'Supreme Dark'

HARDINESS: USDA zones 5–9

ORIGIN: introduced by Thomas DeBaggio and named after his father-in-law, W. K. Doyle; has darker flowers than 'Irene Doyle'

HABIT, HEIGHT × WIDTH: compact but loose and open, 30 × 42 inches (75 × 107 cm)

STEM LENGTH: 10–12 inches (25–30 cm)

SPACING: 36–42 inches (90–107 cm)

FLOWER COLOR: violet to violet-blue, RHS 88A to 89A; despite the name, variation in colors in the corolla gives an overall effect of light violet; buds show white at start of bloom.

FOLIAGE COLOR: gray-green

BLOOMS: twice; early summer and fall

SCENT: rich and sweet

USES: landscape, fresh-cut and dried bundles (dries light in color), culinary

ALTERNATIVES: 'Irene Doyle', 'French Fields'

🟣 *Lavandula angustifolia* 'French Fields'

This very hardy lavender has a prolific bloom during both summer and fall months, making it especially beneficial to fall pollinators.

HARDINESS: USDA zones 5–9

ORIGIN: unknown; resembles wild cultivated lavender; was offered by Van Hevelingen Herb Nursery in Newberg, Oregon, and a nursery in Washington many years ago, with original label, "From the perfume fields of France," then renamed 'French Fields'

HABIT, HEIGHT × WIDTH: compact mound, 30 × 30 inches (75 × 76 cm)

STEM LENGTH: 12–14 inches (30–36 cm)

SPACING: 30–36 inches (76–90 cm)

FLOWER COLOR: mid lavender-violet, RHS 92A

FOLIAGE COLOR: gray-green

BLOOMS: twice, in late spring and early fall

SCENT: highly fragrant

USES: landscape, fresh bouquets, culinary, essential oil

ALTERNATIVES: 'Gray Lady'

🟣🟣 *Lavandula angustifolia* 'True Munstead'

Also known as 'Dwarf Munstead', 'Munstead Blue', 'Munstead Variety'

'True Munstead' is difficult to find, though you may find it occasionally in small, specialized nurseries. It continues to be grown from seed in many nurseries around the world, and many variations are available. Commonly you will find 'Munstead' in large garden centers.

HARDINESS: USDA zones 5–9

ORIGIN: raised by Gertrude Jekyll in the UK and introduced by Barr in 1916

HABIT, HEIGHT × WIDTH: medium-size bushy plant with dense foliage, 20 × 30 inches (50 × 76 cm)

STEM LENGTH: 6–8 inches (15–20 cm)

SPACING: 24–30 inches (60–76 cm)

FLOWER COLOR: mid violet, RHS 86B, to bright violet, RHS 90B–C

FOLIAGE COLOR: mid green

BLOOMS: twice, late spring or early summer and again in fall

SCENT: sweet

USES: landscape, fresh-cut and dried bundles, culinary

ALTERNATIVES: 'Avice Hill', 'Compacta', 'Bowles Early'

PINK FLOWERS

🟣 *Lavandula angustifolia* 'Coconut Ice'

'Coconut Ice' is a two-toned lavender, having both white and pink flowers on the same stem. It is named after the Australasian sweet fudge made of pink- and white-colored sugar.

HARDINESS: USDA zones 5–9

ORIGIN: raised in New Zealand by Virginia McNaughton and released in 1997

HABIT, HEIGHT × WIDTH: compact and upright, 24 × 24 inches (60 × 60 cm)

STEM LENGTH: 8–10 inches (20–25 cm)

SPACING: 24 inches (60 cm)

FLOWER COLOR: mid pink mauve, RHS 75A, or white; before flowering, buds show a pale green

FOLIAGE COLOR: gray-green

BLOOMS: once, early summer

SCENT: mildly sweet

USES: landscape, container

ALTERNATIVES: 'Melissa'

Lavandula angustifolia 'Hidcote Pink'

One of my all-around favorites for fragrance, 'Hidcote Pink' is one to consider if you are a home distiller or would like to scale up your distillation or make perfume.

HARDINESS: USDA zones 5–9

ORIGIN: introduced by Major Lawrence Johnston of Hidcote Manor, Gloucestershire, before 1958 and received an RHS Highly Commended award in 1963; part of the Hidcote Group, which were originally brought to England from France by Major Johnston in the 1920s

HABIT, HEIGHT × WIDTH: compact, medium size, 30 × 36 inches (75 × 90 cm)

STEM LENGTH: 8–12 inches (20–30 cm)

SPACING: 30–36 inches (76–90 cm)

FLOWER COLOR: off pink, RHS 69B, or pale mauve pink, RHS 76C; matures to mid pink mauve, RHS 77C

FOLIAGE COLOR: gray-green

BLOOMS: once, early summer; dense and even bloom

SCENT: sweetly fragrant

USES: landscape (hedging and mass plantings), culinary, perfume, essential oil, hydrosol

ALTERNATIVES: 'Rosea', 'Jean Davis'

Lavandula angustifolia 'Melissa'

Also known as 'Melissa Pink White'

HARDINESS: USDA zones 5–9

ORIGIN: developed by Van Hevelingen Herb Nursery, Newberg, Oregon, by selecting a sport off of a 'Compacta' seedling in 1994, and introduced to the trade in 1999; named after cofounder Melissa Van Hevelingen

HABIT, HEIGHT × WIDTH: tight, compact mound, 20 × 24 inches (50 × 60 cm)

STEM LENGTH: 8–12 inches (20–30 cm)

SPACING: 30 inches (76 cm)

FLOWER COLOR: opening white, maturing to off pink, RHS 69B, with soft pink mauve center, RHS 75B

FOLIAGE COLOR: mid green to gray-green

BLOOMS: once, early summer

SCENT: sweetly fragrant

USES: landscape, container, culinary, with a hint of a peppery note in flavor

ALTERNATIVES: 'Coconut Ice'

Lavandula angustifolia 'Miss Katherine'

Of all the pink cultivars, this is my favorite. Its long stems and resistance to shattering make it ideal for arranging in both fresh and dried bouquets. It contrasts brilliantly with dark violets and autumn colors.

HARDINESS: USDA zones 5–9

ORIGIN: raised by Norfolk Lavender, Norfolk, in 1992, and awarded an RHS Award of Garden Merit in 2002

HABIT, HEIGHT × WIDTH: semi-tall and bushy with long and sturdy stems, 30 × 36 inches (75 × 90 cm)

STEM LENGTH: 12–14 inches (30–36 cm)

SPACING: 36–42 inches (90–107 cm)

FLOWER COLOR: mid pink mauve, RHS 75A, to off gray-pink, RHS 69D, with overtones of mauve-violet and a speck of red in the center of the corolla; one of the darkest of the pink lavenders

FOLIAGE COLOR: gray-green

BLOOMS: once in the late spring or early summer

SCENT: sweet and spicy, very fragrant

USES: landscape, fresh-cut and dried bundles, crafting (sturdy stems and tight calyxes make them shatter-free), culinary, essential oil

ALTERNATIVES: 'Little Lottie' ('Clarmo'), 'Lodden Pink'

WHITE FLOWERS

◯ *Lavandula angustifolia* 'Nana Alba'

Also known as 'Dwarf White', 'Baby White', 'Munstead Alba'

HARDINESS: USDA zones 5–9

ORIGIN: believed to have originated in the UK; earliest mention, 1928

HABIT, HEIGHT × WIDTH: extremely compact, dense and strong, 20 × 24 inches (50 × 60 cm)

STEM LENGTH: 6–8 inches (15–20 cm)

SPACING: 24 inches (60 cm)

FLOWER COLOR: white, with abundant flowers

FOLIAGE COLOR: gray-green

BLOOMS: once, early summer

SCENT: sweet

USES: landscape (beautiful combined with violet-blue cultivars such as 'Thumbelina Leigh' or 'Royal Velvet' in a rock garden or border), container, culinary, essential oil, hydrosol

ALTERNATIVES: 'Purity', 'Alpine White', 'Blue Mountain White', 'White Early', 'BeeZee White'

Lavandula ×intermedia

Lavandula ×intermedia is a sterile hybrid cross, or intermediate, between *L. angustifolia* (true lavender) and *L. latifolia* (spike lavender). In English, Spanish, and French it is commonly referred to as *lavandin*, in Italian as *lavandino*, and in German *Spiklavendel*. This hybrid cross is cold-hardy, and most of the cultivars listed here can be grown at higher elevations and have proven to withstand cold temperatures. Lavandins are also highly resistant to sudden wilt.

The essential oil of spike lavender is big in camphor compounds, giving a fresher scent as compared to true lavenders, which have only trace amounts of camphor. When the two species are crossed, the chemical composition of the plant's essential oil is quite distinct. Some lavandin cultivars, such as 'Super', have less camphor, with their oil producing sweet notes resembling those of a true lavender. Oil production from lavandins is much higher than from true lavender thanks to their large growth habit and large flower heads.

Due to their characteristically long and dramatic stems, lavandin cultivars make ideal fresh and dried flower bouquets. The stems also make these cultivars a showpiece in the garden, perhaps as a hedge along a pathway or home entrance walkway. Lavandins hold their green and silver foliage color during the winter months, again making them ideal for landscaping and hedges.

VIOLET FLOWERS

● *Lavandula* ×*intermedia* 'Gros Bleu'

Also known as 'Tete Carree', 'Square Head'

HARDINESS: USDA zones 5–9

ORIGIN: unknown but has been grown since the late 1940s in France

HABIT, HEIGHT × WIDTH: large, bushy to spherical, 42 × 48 inches (107 × 122 cm)

STEM LENGTH: 18–20 inches (45–51 cm)

SPACING: 36–48 inches (90–122 cm)

FLOWER COLOR: dark violet, RHS 83A, with dark blue woolly calyxes

FOLIAGE COLOR: gray-green

BLOOMS: once, midsummer and late summer

SCENT: clean, light, and fresh

USES: landscape, fresh-cut bouquets, crafting (using buds in sachets and potpourri), culinary (flavoring beverages through infusion)

ALTERNATIVES: 'Olympia', 'Downoly'

LAVENDER FOR ALL SEASONS

● ● *Lavandula* ×*intermedia* 'Grosso'

Also known as 'Dilly Dilly', 'Wilson's Giant'

HARDINESS: USDA zones 5–9; can be grown at higher elevations but is prone to winter dieback in colder climates

ORIGIN: discovered in 1972 by Pierre Grosso, a farmer in Goult, France, who propagated sturdy plants that were growing in an abandoned field and found them to be quite vigorous and high yielding; neighboring farmers obtained cuttings and production exploded, at one time making up at least 10 percent of the lavandin crop in France; with high oil yields competitive with newer lavandin cultivars in the market today

HABIT, HEIGHT × WIDTH: dense, compact bush with stems splayed out 180 degrees, 36 × 62 inches (90 × 158 cm)

STEM LENGTH: 18–20 inches (45–51 cm)

SPACING: 36–62 inches (90–158 cm)

FLOWER COLOR: vibrant to soft violet, RHS 86A, or vibrant violet, RHS 88A

FOLIAGE COLOR: gray-green

BLOOMS: once, mid-to-late summer, long lasting

SCENT: pungent, herbaceous, camphorous

USES: landscape (hedging), fresh-cut bundles, crafting (using buds in potpourri), essential oil, hydrosol

ALTERNATIVES: 'Abrialii' (a little smaller and shorter stems), 'Impress Purple', 'Niko'

● *Lavandula* ×*intermedia* 'Impress Purple'

Also known as '41/70', 'Arabian Night'

In my experience, 'Impress Purple' makes nice dried-flower bundles. The buds tend not to shatter as much as their counterparts, and it maintains an attractive dark slate purple color when dried.

HARDINESS: USDA zones 5–9; tends to be hardier than its counterpart 'Grosso'

ORIGIN: '41/70', a French field variety imported into New Zealand in 1983 and renamed 'Impress Purple' in 1994 by Peter Smale

HABIT, HEIGHT × WIDTH: bushy with sprawling stems, moderately dense, 40 × 60 inches (100 × 150 cm)

STEM LENGTH: 20 inches (51 cm)

SPACING: 36–42 inches (90–107 cm)

FLOWER COLOR: vibrant violet, RHS 88A, fading to mid violet, one of the darkest lavandins

FOLIAGE COLOR: gray-green

BLOOMS: once, midsummer, long lasting

SCENT: slightly camphorous with a hint of sweet

USES: landscape, fresh-cut and dried bundles, crafting (using buds in sachets), essential oil, hydrosol

ALTERNATIVES: 'Grosso'

VIOLET-BLUE FLOWERS

● *Lavandula* ×*intermedia* 'Hidcote Giant'

HARDINESS: USDA zones 5–9

ORIGIN: raised by Major Lawrence Johnston of Hidcote Manor, Gloucester, sometime before 1957; awarded the RHS Award of Garden Merit in 1984 and 2001; member of the Hidcote Giant Group, whose members have a distinctive thick, conical, blocky base, with slightly blunt-ended spikes

HABIT, HEIGHT × WIDTH: large, compact bush with long stems and large flower heads, 42 × 48 inches (107 × 122 cm)

STEM LENGTH: 14–18 inches (36–45 cm)

SPACING: 42–48 inches (107–122 cm)

FLOWER COLOR: bright violet-blue, RHS 90B

FOLIAGE COLOR: gray-green

BLOOMS: once, midsummer

SCENT: slightly sweet, strong fragrance

USES: landscape (hedging), fresh-cut and dried bundles, crafting

ALTERNATIVES: 'Pale Pretender', 'Walberton's Silver Edge'

SELECTING YOUR PLANTS

● *Lavandula* ×*intermedia* 'Niko'

Also known by the trade name Phenomenal (PP24193)

HARDINESS: USDA zones 5–9; tolerates extreme heat and humidity

ORIGIN: selected by Lloyd and Candy Traven of Peace Tree Farms in Kintnersville, Pennsylvania, in 2012, who noted this sport (whole plant mutation) growing in a crop of *Lavandula ×intermedia* 'Grosso' at their nursery; received US plant patent in January 2014 using the cultivar name 'Niko' after one of their customers, Niko Christou; was selected for its compact and rounded habit, winter hardiness, and disease resistance (particularly to *Pythium* fungus species)

HABIT, HEIGHT × WIDTH: upright and compact, strong vigor, 30 × 36 inches (76 × 90 cm)

STEM LENGTH: 18–20 inches (45–51 cm)

SPACING: 36–42 inches (90–107 cm)

FLOWER COLOR: violet-blue, RHS 90D

FOLIAGE COLOR: gray-green

BLOOMS: once, late spring, early summer, or midsummer; long lasting

SCENT: strong, pungent, and herbaceous

USES: landscape (hedging), fresh-cut and dried bundles, crafting (potpourri)

ALTERNATIVES: 'Impress Purple', 'Grosso'

● *Lavandula ×intermedia* 'Provence'

Also known as 'Du Provence'

Commonly available in large garden centers, especially ones in more temperate climates.

HARDINESS: USDA zones 7–9; is prone to fungal disease in wetter climates but does well in moderate and dry climates

ORIGIN: named for the famous lavender-growing region of France but thought to have originated at Alpenglow Gardens, North Surrey, British Columbia, in the 1950s, with the first plant shipped into the United States in 1965

HABIT, HEIGHT × WIDTH: erect bush with vigorous growth, 42 × 54 inches (107 × 137 cm)

STEM LENGTH: 24 inches (60 cm)

SPACING: 42–54 inches (107–137 cm)

FLOWER COLOR: lavender-violet, RHS 94C

FOLIAGE COLOR: gray-green

BLOOMS: mid-to-late summer with sporadic blooms in fall

SCENT: sweet floral

USES: landscape, fresh-cut bundles (less suitable for dried, as buds shatter), crafting (potpourri), culinary (good in dishes and tea blends, as one of the mildest lavandins)

ALTERNATIVES: 'Tuscan'

SELECTING YOUR PLANTS

● *Lavandula* ×*intermedia* 'Riverina Thomas'

Also known as 'CSU150'

HARDINESS: USDA zones 5–9

ORIGIN: developed in 2009 in the breeding program of Dr. Nigel Urwin of Charles Sturt University in the Riverina agricultural region of New South Wales, Australia; a triploid hybrid (meaning it has an added chromosome) created by crossing the lavandin 'Grosso' with a nonspecified true lavender; among the world's first commercially available polyploid lavenders, which Dr. Urwin reported "should be higher yielding and produce equivalent or better-quality oils than currently grown varieties"

HABIT, HEIGHT × WIDTH: upright compact mound, vigorous grower with long, tapered flower spikes, 30 × 36 inches (76 × 90 cm)

STEM LENGTH: 14–26 inches (36–66 cm), exceptionally long, sturdy stems as well as long lateral stems

SPACING: 36–42 inches (90–107 cm)

FLOWER COLOR: bright violet-blue, RHS 90B

FOLIAGE COLOR: gray-green

BLOOMS: once, midsummer, long lasting, with a slight secondary bloom in fall

SCENT: slightly sweet, spicy, and slightly woody

USES: landscape (hedging), fresh-cut and dried bundles, crafting (potpourri), essential oil, hydrosol

ALTERNATIVES: 'Riverina Alan' (an even larger version of 'Riverina Thomas'), 'Impress Purple'

🟣 *Lavandula* ×*intermedia* 'Seal'

HARDINESS: USDA zones 5–9

ORIGIN: field-selected in 1935 by Miss D. G. Hewer of the Herb Farm and raised in Seal, United Kingdom; one of the Mitcham Group, large essential oil producers

HABIT, HEIGHT × WIDTH: moderately dense and bushy with long lateral branches, 36 × 36 inches (90 × 90 cm)

STEM LENGTH: 18–20 inches (45–51 cm)

SPACING: 36–42 inches (90–107 cm)

FLOWER COLOR: violet-blue, RHS 90C

FOLIAGE COLOR: gray-green

BLOOMS: once, mid-to-late summer

SCENT: soft and pleasant, long-lasting

USES: landscape (hedging), fresh-cut bundles, crafting (potpourri), essential oil, hydrosol

ALTERNATIVES: 'Alba', 'Bogong', 'Grappenhall'

● *Lavandula* ×*intermedia* 'Super'

Also known as 'Super A', 'Super AA', 'Super B'

At my farm, this is the last of the lavenders to harvest and distill for the essential oil and hydrosol, a wonderful benchmark that tells me the lavender season is coming to an end. One of my favorite lavandins not only in form and function but also for its vigorous rooting qualities, which make it easy to propagate.

HARDINESS: USDA zones 5–9

ORIGIN: introduced in various versions in the 1950s and 1960s in France, so that 'Super' is a generic term for a class of lavandins, including several clones that fall within commercially accepted standards for this cultivar, such as 'Sussex' and 'Walvera'

HABIT, HEIGHT × WIDTH: large, moderately dense and bushy, 52 × 60 inches (132 × 150 cm)

STEM LENGTH: 18–24 inches (45–60 cm)

SPACING: 48–52 inches (122–132 cm)

FLOWER COLOR: violet-blue, RHS 90C

FOLIAGE COLOR: gray-green

BLOOMS: once, mid-to-late summer, long-lasting

SCENT: light, floral, and sweet, resembling that of a true lavender

USES: landscape, fresh-cut and dried bundles, essential oil, hydrosol

ALTERNATIVES: 'Seal'

Opposite: Author in between nine-year-old *Lavandula* ×*intermedia* 'Super' to the left and three-year-old 'Super' to the right.

94 LAVENDER FOR ALL SEASONS

WHITE FLOWERS

◯ *Lavandula* ×*intermedia* 'Edelweiss'

Also known as 'Snow Cap', 'Grosso White'

Among the hardiest of all lavandins I have grown. Separated whorls make the flower heads long and stunning. Beautiful when grown alongside 'Gros Bleu', creating a striking contrast of color as they both bloom at the same time.

HARDINESS: USDA zones 5–9

ORIGIN: first appeared in the 1980s in Europe, making it one of the more recent white-flowered lavandins; similar to white 'Grosso' cultivars that were introduced in France and the United Kingdom during that time

HABIT, HEIGHT × WIDTH: large and sprawling well-shaped bush, 36 × 54 inches (90 × 137 cm)

STEM LENGTH: 18–20 inches (45–51 cm)

SPACING: 42–72 inches (107–183 cm)

FLOWER COLOR: pure white with a slight tint of gray

FOLIAGE COLOR: gray-green

BLOOMS: once, mid-to-late summer, long-lasting

SCENT: sweet and pleasant

USES: landscape (hedging), fresh-cut and dried bundles, crafting, essential oil, hydrosol

ALTERNATIVES: 'Alba' (more compact flower heads; not to be confused with the true lavender 'Nana Alba'), 'Hidcote White', 'Caty Blanc', 'Exceptional'

Lavandula ×chaytorae

Lavandula ×chaytorae is a cross between *L. angustifolia* and *L. lanata*. *Lavandula lanata* is known for its woolly silver-gray foliage and gray calyxes that contrast brilliantly with its dark purple corollas. This unique trait is not lost in this hybrid cross. The plant proves noteworthy in any garden, showing its beauty with or without flowers. It blooms in shades of violet and violet-blue, and the leaves contrast well with neighboring plants blooming in colors of red, yellow, and pink, and with foliage in shades of dark and bright green. *Lavandula ×chaytorae* is generally not as hardy as true lavender or lavandins, but nonetheless a few cultivars do well in colder climates.

● *Lavandula* ×*chaytorae* 'Ana Luisa'

This cultivar, which is larger than 'Kathleen Elizabeth', has proven to withstand colder temperatures. I have had it growing on our farm for sixteen years, withstanding many harsh winters. Maintains silver foliage even during the cold months.

HARDINESS: USDA zones 6–10

ORIGIN: introduced by Van Hevelingen Herb Nursery in Newberg, Oregon, in 1998

HABIT, HEIGHT × WIDTH: moderately dense and bushy, 36 × 35 inches (90 × 90 cm)

STEM LENGTH: 18–20 inches (45–51 cm)

SPACING: 36–42 inches (90–107 cm)

FLOWER COLOR: dark violet, RHS 83A

FOLIAGE COLOR: silver-gray

BLOOMS: once, early-to-mid summer

SCENT: sweet, highly fragrant

USES: landscape (hedging), fresh-cut bundles

ALTERNATIVES: 'Kathleen Elizabeth'

● *Lavandula* ×*chaytorae* 'Lisa Marie'

HARDINESS: USDA zones 6–10

ORIGIN: developed in 1991 by Kenneth Montgomery of Anderson Valley Nursery, Boonville, California; gets its compact habit and hardiness from its parent *Lavandula angustifolia* 'Martha Roderick' and its silvery foliage and violet corollas from *L. lanata*

HABIT, HEIGHT × WIDTH: compact mound with long lateral branches, 36 × 36 inches (90 × 90 cm)

STEM LENGTH: 12–15 inches (30–38 cm)

SPACING: 36–42 inches (90–107 cm)

FLOWER COLOR: violet-blue, RHS 89B

FOLIAGE COLOR: silver

BLOOMS: once, early-to-mid summer

SCENT: very fragrant

USES: landscape (hedging), fresh-cut bundles, crafting

ALTERNATIVES: 'Jennifer'

● *Lavandula* ×*chaytorae* 'Richard Gray'

HARDINESS: USDA zones 6–10; will tolerate as low as zone 5

ORIGIN: discovered as a seedling at Royal Botanic Gardens, Kew, in the 1980s and introduced commercially in the 1990s

HABIT, HEIGHT × WIDTH: dense and compact, older plants spreading but upright, 20 × 28 inches (51 × 71 cm)

STEM LENGTH: 10–12 inches (25–30 cm)

SPACING: 30 inches (76 cm)

FLOWER COLOR: vibrant violet, RHS 88A

FOLIAGE COLOR: silver

BLOOMS: once, early-to-mid summer, short spikes

SCENT: sweetly pungent

USES: landscape (in front of garden beds), fresh-cut bundles

ALTERNATIVES: 'Jennifer', 'England'

Lavandula stoechas

Lavandula stoechas was the first recognized lavender, mentioned in writings dating from about 65 CE. The word *stoechas* is derived from the Stoechas Islands, now known as Îles d'Hyères, off the southern coast of France near Toulon. In English, *L. stoechas* is commonly referred to as French or Spanish lavender; in Spanish as *estecados*, in French as *lavande stéchas*, and in Italian as *steca*. To avoid any confusion, I like to refer to this species as just stoechas (pronounced STOW-kass).

This species was used extensively by the Romans and the Greeks, who valued it highly for its medicinal properties. *Lavandula stoechas* is known for its anti-inflammatory and antimicrobial properties. The flowers and leaves combined are high in fenchone, a terpene that contributes to its woodsy and earthy aroma. Today, stoechas is grown on a small scale for oil but is more commonly grown and valued as an ornamental. Blooms come in many different shades on the spectrum between red-purple and violet-blue, including dark reddish purple, dark violet, electric dark blue, and dark purple-mauve.

This frost-hardy species will survive a few degrees of frost, but it thrives in warm, humid climates and does not require a period of winter cold to flower well. It is known to bloom year-round in greenhouse conditions. In colder climates, below USDA zone 7, it needs a frost-free environment and should be given protection during the winter months. In my zone, 6, I grow stoechas in terra cotta pots that I bring inside before the first frost in fall. Since these lavenders are not commonly found in Colorado, they are always a conversation piece because of their "rabbit ears," which are actually the plant's sterile bracts.

If you grow *L. stoechas* in pots, be sure to give it ample room and replant or pot up every three years to get plenty of fresh blooms. Whether you grow it in pots or in the ground, you will enjoy this plant in its first growing season due to its fast growth and abundant bloom. It will bloom throughout the season if you remove all dead flower heads and trim off about a third of the plant. Stoechas are known to self-seed. You may find tiny plants starting at the base of the plant.

Lavandula stoechas has multiple subspecies, one of the most common being *stoechas*. Some of the well-known cultivars in this subspecies include 'Liberty', 'Lilac Wings', 'Provencal', 'Otto Quast', and 'Kew Red'. Another subspecies is *pedunculata*, or butterfly lavender, distinguished by its wispy apical bracts that resemble butterflies fluttering above. Because of its beauty, *L. stoechas* subsp. *pedunculata* is considered the most gardenworthy of all lavenders. Common cultivars include 'Atlas', 'James Compton', and 'Papillon'.

Within *L. stoechas* are multitudes of hybrids resulting from cross-pollination. Some of those hybrids are crosses with *Lavandula viridis* or green lavender, also known as *L. stoechas* 'Viridis'. This lavender is known for its white or green floral bracts. These attract not only bees during the day but also night-flying pollinators like moths, making this species an amazing pollinator plant to have in your garden or greenhouse. One example of a cross between *L. stoechas* and *L. viridis* is 'Ballerina'.

An old metal watering can makes a fine planter for *Lavandula stoechas* 'Victory'.

● *Lavandula stoechas* 'Anouk'

HARDINESS: USDA zones 6–10

ORIGIN: planned breeding program conducted by Lammert Koning in the Netherlands in 2002; patent PP16685 granted in 2006

HABIT, HEIGHT × WIDTH: compact with outward and upright branches, 36 × 30 inches (90 × 76 cm)

STEM LENGTH: 2–4 inches (5–10 cm)

SPACING: 30 inches (76 cm)

FLOWER COLOR: deep dark violet, RHS 83A to 83B

FOLIAGE COLOR: mid green to gray-green

BLOOMS: continuous, late spring to late summer

SCENT: pungent

USES: landscape (hedging), containers

ALTERNATIVES: 'Anouk Twilight', 'Anouk Supreme'

● *Lavandula stoechas* 'Regal Splendour'

Also known as 'Regal Splendor'

    This cultivar is considered a hybrid cross of *L. pedunculata* and *L. viridis* but is sold under the umbrella of *L. stoechas*. To maintain a compact shape, prune regularly. Thrives best in frost-free regions but will tolerate lower temperatures and can be considered frost-hardy.

HARDINESS: USDA zones 7b–9a

ORIGIN: developed by Marilyn and Ian Wightman of New Zealand in 1994; introduced to the UK in 2001

HABIT, HEIGHT × WIDTH: upright and bushy, 30 × 36 inches (76 × 90 cm)

STEM LENGTH: 2–4 inches (5–10 cm)

SPACING: 30–36 inches (76–90 cm)

FLOWER COLOR: electric dark blue, RHS 89A; apical bracts vibrant mauve

FOLIAGE COLOR: bright green

BLOOMS: continuous, spring through summer

SCENT: pungent

USES: landscape (hedging), containers

ALTERNATIVES: 'Wings of Night'

● *Lavandula stoechas* subsp. *pedunculata* 'James Compton'

Also known as 'Butterfly', 'Fairy Wings', *L. pedunculata* 'James Compton'

HARDINESS: USDA zones 7–10

ORIGIN: grown from seed collected by Jamie Compton on the hillside between Almeria and Granada, Spain, in about 1979; one of the earliest named cultivars, with newer selections replacing many since then

HABIT, HEIGHT × WIDTH: upright, 36 × 36 inches (90 × 90 cm)

STEM LENGTH: 8 inches (20 cm)

SPACING: 30–36 inches (76–90 cm)

FLOWER COLOR: dark purple-black corolla; apical bracts dark purple-mauve, RHS 77A, with red-purple midribs

FOLIAGE COLOR: gray-green

BLOOMS: continuous, late spring to late summer

SCENT: pungent

USES: landscape (hedging)

ALTERNATIVES: 'Papillon', 'Portuguese Giant', 'Purple Crown', 'Wine Red'

●● ● *Lavandula stoechas* subsp. *stoechas* f. *rosea* 'Kew Red'

Also known as 'Kew Pink', 'Red Kew'

HARDINESS: USDA zones 7–10

ORIGIN: raised from a cutting from a plant grown in Almira, Spain

HABIT, HEIGHT × WIDTH: compact and upright, 18 × 18 inches (45 × 45 cm)

STEM LENGTH: 2–3 inches (5–7.6 cm)

SPACING: 18–24 inches (45–60 cm)

FLOWER COLOR: cerise crimson corollas, mid to dark reddish purple, RHS 71A–72A; apical bracts soft pink, RHS 65B

FOLIAGE COLOR: mid green to gray-green

BLOOMS: continuous, late spring to late summer

SCENT: mild

USES: landscape, containers

ALTERNATIVES: 'Peter Pink', 'Pierre's Pink'

●● *Lavandula stoechas* ×*viridis* 'Ballerina'

Also known as 'Ploughman's Ballerina'

HARDINESS: USDA zones 7–10

ORIGIN: hybrid cross raised by Peter Carter of Ploughman's Garden and Nursery, New Zealand, in 1997

HABIT, HEIGHT × WIDTH: upright, 24 × 24 inches (60 × 60 cm)

STEM LENGTH: 6–7 inches (15–18 cm)

SPACING: 18–24 inches (45–60 cm)

FLOWER COLOR: corollas dark violet, RHS 83A; apical bracts white with green midribs, maturing to mauve-violet, RHS 84A

FOLIAGE COLOR: mid green to gray-green

BLOOMS: continuous, late spring to late summer

SCENT: pungent, camphorous

USES: landscape, containers

ALTERNATIVES: 'Crème Brûlée', 'Madrid Blue'

● *Lavandula viridis*

Also known *Lavandula stoechas* 'Viridis', green lavender

HARDINESS: USDA zones 7–10

ORIGIN: native to southwest Spain and southern Portugal

HABIT, HEIGHT × WIDTH: upright, 36 × 36 inches (90 × 90 cm)

STEM LENGTH: 12 inches (30 cm)

SPACING: 36–42 inches (90–107 cm)

FLOWER COLOR: white to greenish white with greenish-white bracts, RHS 150C

FOLIAGE COLOR: very green

BLOOMS: continuous, late spring to late summer

SCENT: pungent to lemony

USES: landscape (use to contrast with deep purples)

Lavandula dentata

Lavandula dentata dates back more than a thousand years, with the first record of it published in the eleventh century. *Dentata* means "toothed," which describes the plant's leaf, having indentations that look like a row of teeth. *Lavandula dentata* was first classified as a member of *L. stoechas* due to its having bracts at the apex of its spike. In fact, *L. dentata* bracts are part of the spike, and there are just a few completely sterile bracts at the top. The plant was reclassified as a separate species in 1946, and later Tim Upson clarified that based on morphological and molecular data, this species should indeed be classified separately. Two varieties are recognized: *L. dentata* var. *dentata* and *L. dentata* var. *candicans*. The former has gray-green leaves, the latter silver-gray leaves.

Common names vary around the world. In Australia and Europe it is referred to as fringed lavender or toothed lavender. In the United States, it is often referred to as French lavender; in France as *lavande dentée*, in Spain as *alhucema rizada*, in Germany as *Gezähnter Lavendel*, and in India as *ustukhuddus*.

My first experience with *Lavandula dentata* was in the coastal hills of northern California. I worked on a farm that was terraced along a steep hillside, so the only way to tend the plants was by using horse-drawn plows and cultivators. The plants grew into a gray-green hedge and bloomed pale blue-violet for most of the year. With a balsamy scent like rosemary with a hint of lavender, this species was used to replace rosemary and accent plates in upscale San Francisco restaurants. Since then, I have learned there are more pleasant-tasting species, yet *L. dentata* is still beautiful adorning plates and dried in potpourri and sachets. Medicinally it has many of the same qualities as *L. stoechas*.

This half-hardy species is well suited for sunny borders, hedges, and containers in frost-free climates and is known to bloom year-round in drought-free conditions. What is so amazing is this species can grow at sea level but is also known to grow in the highlands of Ethiopia and Eritrea in East Africa at an elevation of 3000 meters (9842 feet). There is a pink-flowered variation, *L. dentata* var. *dentata* f. *rosea*, grown in Morocco and Saudi Arabia.

● *Lavandula dentata*

HARDINESS: USDA zones 9b–12a

ORIGIN: unknown, but most likely somewhere in Algeria, Baleares, Eritrea, Ethiopia, Morocco, Palestine, Saudi Arabia, Spain, or Yemen

HABIT, HEIGHT × WIDTH: compact with outward and upright branches, 24 × 30 inches (60 × 76 cm)

STEM LENGTH: 6–8 inches (15–20 cm)

SPACING: 30 inches (76 cm)

FLOWER COLOR: light violet to blue violet

FOLIAGE COLOR: green to gray-green

BLOOMS: once, late spring to early summer; in certain conditions can bloom year-round

SCENT: pungent, like eucalyptus

USES: landscape (hedging), containers, crafting (potpourri)

ALTERNATIVES: *L. dentata* var. *dentata* 'Linda Ligon', *L. dentata* var. *dentata* 'Dusky Maiden'

Lavandula ×*allardii* and *Lavandula* ×*heterophylla*

Lavandula ×*allardii* is the product of a spontaneous cross between *L. dentata* and *L. latifolia* that occurred in Angers, France. *Lavandula* ×*heterophylla* is thought to be a cross between *L. dentata* and *L. angustifolia*. Both tender species are best suited to frost-free climates and can withstand hot and humid summers. Cultivated for ornamental use, they are similar to lavandins and latifolias in appearance and make great borders and hedges due to their large size and long flower spikes, though the bloom period is short compared to other lavender varieties. Leaves at the base of the plants are toothed, while higher leaves have smooth margins. Regular pruning after flowering is needed to ensure these plants do not look untidy.

Lavandula ×*allardii*

Also known as heterophylla lavender, heterophylla fringed lavender, Allard's lavender

HARDINESS: USDA zone 10

ORIGIN: grown in Mediterranean and subtropical landscapes; popular in Australia, New Zealand, neighboring Pacific Ocean islands, South Africa, Mediterranean Europe, and Madeira

HABIT, HEIGHT × WIDTH: large (can be giant) and bushy with outward and upright branches, 30 × 36 inches (76 × 90 cm)

STEM LENGTH: 14–18 inches (36–45 cm)

SPACING: 36–54 inches (90–137 cm)

FLOWER COLOR: light purple to violet-blue, RHS 79C to RHS 90C, depending on the hybrid

FOLIAGE COLOR: gray-green

BLOOMS: once, late spring to early summer; in certain conditions can bloom year-round

SCENT: pungent, notes of camphor and eucalyptus

USES: landscape (hedging), containers, fresh-cut bundles

ALTERNATIVES: modern hybrid clones 'African Pride' and 'Anzac Pride', 'Meerlo' (variegated foliage)

Chapter 3

How to Grow and Care for Lavender

Spring and fall are both perfect times to take the first step toward planting a lavender patch of your own. Imagine a terrace garden of lavender in a corner of your yard or a line of voluminous, whimsical lavandin plants along your driveway that greet you when you arrive home. Envision rows of lavender replacing your thirsty lawn with purples, blues, silvers, and pinks, the smell wafting over you when you walk by.

Once established, lavender is a hardy plant that does not require much care. However, for your plants to thrive and produce bountiful flowers and enjoyment for many years, you should understand lavender's needs, beginning with a sunny site and loose, neutral-to-alkaline soil.

Choosing the Right Site

Lavender requires a minimum of six hours a day of full sun. Your best site to plant lavender is on a south-facing hillside or slope in full sun. This replicates how lavender grows in the wild. If that cannot be achieved, site plants where they will get at least six to eight hours of full sun daily. Anything under and your plants will not thrive or reach their potential.

Hardy lavender can withstand more exposed locations. Frost-hardy lavender grows in temperatures as low as 5 to 30 degrees F (–15 to –1 degree C) but also requires some shelter. Lavender plants can be sheltered by structures or windbreaks. Growing a row of ornamental grasses or evergreens that can block cold winds is ideal. Half-hardy lavenders can be grown in frost-free zones. They also can be kept in a greenhouse or sunroom during winter. Tender lavenders can survive and thrive year-round in more temperate climates.

Lavender does well growing with other drought-tolerant plants or in a xeriscape environment like a rock garden, where conditions are dry with little wind. Later in this chapter you will find suggestions for companion planting.

Lavender Care Through the Seasons

Each season will bring you a few tasks to do when growing and maintaining lavender. Here is a summary of what to do when.

LAVENDER CARE THROUGH THE SEASONS

Task	Winter	Spring	Summer	Fall
Plan and prepare soil		all zones		all zones
Plant		USDA zones 5 to 10		USDA zones 7 and above
Fertilize		all zones		all zones
Prune		USDA zones below zone 7		USDA zones 7 and above
Protect	all zones			

Preparing Your Soil

Good drainage is fundamental for growing lavender. The best soil for lavender is sandy loam or naturally well-drained soil. This type of soil has large particles mixed with small particles, creating a loose soil structure that is ideal for water, air, and roots to move through. Clay soil, by contrast, does not drain well; it is composed of very fine mineral particles and not much organic material to create space between the mineral particles. A clay-loam soil drains better but is still challenging. Sandy soil is the opposite of clay and lacks the ability to maintain soil moisture when needed.

Water enters and drains or percolates through coarse soil most rapidly because of the large pore space. But coarse soil will dry out more quickly and you will have to water more often, plus nutrients will leach out of coarse soils more quickly. Gardeners or growers with fine, clay soils have the opposite problem, poor drainage and excess water as soils dry out much more slowly, but finer soils also retain nutrients better than coarse soils. Sandy soil can lack adequate nutrients as water drains right through.

Your soil structure will dictate how you prepare the area you are planting into. If you do not have the perfect mix of sand, silt, and clay, do not worry. There are things you can do to enhance your soil structure, creating a perfect growing environment for lavender.

Slow-draining soils like heavy clay can be amended with lots of organic matter such as aged compost and volcanic rock. Creating a planting mound or raised bed above the existing soil line can also improve drainage and allow more room for roots to grow. This works well if you have a layer of hardpan (also known as caliche) below the topsoil. I like to create a mound at least 8 inches high and 24 inches wide. To have an even planting surface, smooth and flatten the top of your mound; this will prevent any roots from being exposed. For sandy soil, amending with compost is your friend—it helps retain soil moisture, adds nutrients, and slows drainage.

Lavender likes neutral to alkaline soil, a pH of 6.5 or 7.5, and generally grows well in soil up to a pH of 8.0. If your soil has a pH below 6.5, add dolomite lime and organic compost to bring it up. If it has a pH higher than 8.0, the best way to lower the pH is to add sulfur. Most nurseries sell garden sulfur in the area with compost or fertilizers. Consult the instructions on the bag or box for how much to add, and mix the sulfur well with compost before applying to avoid damaging your garden soil. Generally, you will use more sulfur in clay soil and less in sandy soil. Another

Trading Your Lawn for Lavender

Did you know that the average lawn uses 55,000 gallons of water a year per 1000 square feet? Converting a hundred lawns to low-water-use gardens could save 5.5 million gallons of water a year! There are many options, including sowing lower-water lawn seeds, clover, or native grass mixes, or planting low-growing perennials such as veronica, thyme, Greek yarrow (*Achillea ageratifolia*), or Mount Atlas daisy (*Anacyclus depressus*). You could also try a lavender patch on its own or mixed with compatible low-water, low-maintenance plants.

To include with your lavender, choose native plants along with xeriscape plants and grasses that entice pollinators and beneficial insects, such as the ones mentioned in the "Companion Planting" section later in this chapter. Mix solitary perennial plants like yarrow or Japanese barberry in with lavender or plant a multitude of different perennials with the same growing requirements in a large garden bed.

right: Land previously planted in lawn is now saving water as a lavender patch.

below: Contrasting summer colors of *Lavandula angustifolia* 'Hidcote' and *Berberis thunbergii* 'Atropurpurea Nana' light up a knot garden.

opposite: *Lavandula angustifolia* 'Hidcote' is planted with Japanese sedge, *Carex oshimensis* 'Everlime', which has the same growing requirements.

Know Your Soil

Not sure of your soil structure? Do a percolation test, a super easy procedure that tells you all you need to know about how good your drainage is.

❶ Dig a hole at least 12 inches in diameter by 12 inches deep, with straight sides. If you're testing your entire property, dig several holes scattered throughout your field, since drainage can vary from area to area.

❷ Fill the hole with water and let it sit overnight. This saturates the soil and helps give a more accurate test reading.

❸ The next day, refill the hole with water.

❹ Measure the water level by laying a stick, pipe, or other straightedge across the top of the hole, then measuring with a tape measure or yardstick to determine the distance from the straightedge to the water.

❺ Continue to measure the water level every hour until the hole is empty, noting the number of inches the water level drops per hour.

Ideal soil drainage is about 2 inches per hour. If the rate is less than 1 inch per hour, the drainage is too slow, and if it is more than 4 inches per hour, it's too fast.

I also highly recommend growers at any scale get a soil analysis to understand what is in your soil and what you may need to add. You can use a home kit or your local cooperative extension office to guide you. A soil analysis will help you determine soil density and permeability, structure, amount of organic matter, and presence of essential elements: primary macronutrients, secondary macronutrients, and micronutrients (nutrients in trace amounts). The results of your soil analysis will help you decide whether you'll create raised beds, add more nutrients to the soil, till, or apply lime (calcium carbonate) or gypsum (calcium sulfate).

option to lower soil pH is to add composted wood chips or sawdust, a cost-effective alternative that increases moisture retention, making it especially good for sandy soils. Stay away from composted pine needles, as they can inhibit lavender growth.

The terrain of your garden landscape will also dictate what you may have to do to grow lavender. The soil in my gardens is mainly clay loam, so I have mounded all my growing beds. I also have a terraced landscape that does not require mounding because the lavender is growing on a downward slope, which facilitates good drainage. Before I ever planted my gardens and fields, I amended the soil with compost and rotated cover crops to add organic matter. I have used winter rye for a winter cover crop and a legume, grass, and oat mix as a cover crop in spring.

As I'm always anticipating the current and future growing seasons, my farm is a patchwork of colors and textures.

When to Plant Lavender

Which season to plant in depends on your growing region, your intentions, the resources available to you, and the size of your planting. The best time of year to plant lavender is in spring or fall, though there are pros and cons to each season.

Lavender needs a good eight to ten weeks to get established before soil temperatures get too low or a hard frost arrives. As the soil temperature is increasing in spring, the risk of frost is minimal. On the other hand, in spring plants won't grow until soils are warm enough. Planting into the warm soils of fall allows roots to grow right away, giving them a healthy start. In fall, plants can establish themselves under ideal conditions: warm weather, a less scorching sun, and less pest pressure.

On the left is a field planted in a spring cover crop; on the right, a field newly planted with lavender.

HOW TO GROW AND CARE FOR LAVENDER 117

The progressively cooling temperatures of fall, as opposed to the rising temperatures and erratic weather of spring, help lavender and other perennials transition into the ground. Though lavender is incredibly heat tolerant once established, like many other perennials it does better in cooler temperatures until its roots are established.

Planting in the early fall while the soil is still warm from summer is best in USDA zones 7 and above, or when the plant has at least eight to ten weeks to adapt to and take root in the native soil before the first hard freeze arrives. Knowing your hardiness zone and your region's average first hard frost date can help you determine when to do your fall planting. Count backward eight to ten weeks from the expected first hard frost.

Regarding intention, are you planting a few plants around your house, or a full acre? Risk is a big factor in fall planting. The reward is a head start in spring, but if a hard freeze comes before your plants are fully established, you run the risk of losing some or many of your plants. Fall planting is a more viable option in regions with milder winters. In colder regions, I would try experimenting with a small fall planting before diving into a big planting, to make extra sure the hardier varieties will work well in your region.

How to Plant Lavender

Start with a healthy plant that is suited to your growing zone or microclimate. Before putting your plant into the ground, water your soil until it is moist but not muddy. I recommend having a watering system (even if that just means a full watering can) set up before you plant so that you can water right away after transplanting. If you will be using drip irrigation, irrigate before planting.

Shape your plant start to promote side branching by trimming any flowering stems or shoots that are developing on the plant. (It might seem counterintuitive to remove flowers when they're what you want ultimately, but it helps the plant put energy into its roots, which delivers more bloom in the end.)

Dig a hole twice the size of your plant. Remove the plant from the pot. If roots are tightly packed and growing in a circular form, open up the root-ball a bit with your fingers to ensure the roots will grow outward and downward instead of girdling the plant. Place the plant, with roots open, in the hole. Press the soil down firmly around the roots and water thoroughly.

Plant in well-prepared soil to promote good drainage.

Room to Grow

When you begin with a small, new plant, sometimes it is difficult to imagine how large it will become. Do not be shy about giving the plant some wiggle room. Improper spacing can affect flowering potential. Also, plants need air movement between them to prevent fungal diseases. This is especially the case in warmer, wetter and humid climates.

For *Lavandula ×intermedia* cultivars, allow a minimum of 36 to 52 inches (90 to 132 cm) between plants (measured from the center of one plant to the center of the adjoining plant). For *L. angustifolia* cultivars, plants need to be from 24 to 48 inches (60 to 122 cm) apart. If you want walking space in between where plants are growing, leave a minimum of 5 feet (1.5 m) between them.

Lavandins planted 3 feet apart, the minimum for *Lavandula ×intermedia* cultivars. The plants in the forefront are two years old, and the plants behind me are four years old.

Watering Your Lavender

Lavender is a drought-tolerant plant, but that does not mean it does not need water. Drought-tolerant plants can still experience drought stress, which results in reduced stem length and a reduced number of flower heads. A prolonged amount of drought stress can also have an effect on important chemical compounds in lavender, such as the linalool and linalyl acetate balance. To maximize flower production and plant health, watering to avoid low-water stress is important.

Watering is never straightforward. The best thing to do is to go out in your garden and check your soil moisture by using your finger or a hand trowel. Lightly dig near the root zone to see what the soil feels like to the touch or use a soil moisture meter probe in the root zone to measure soil moisture. The most common mistake in growing lavender is *over*watering. The plant appreciates deep soaks followed by drying out between waterings to 20 percent moisture. Variables that dictate the frequency of watering are your climatic conditions, soil type, stage of plant growth, and stage of flower development.

Climatic conditions such as wind, snow cover (which can act as protection, especially if it is a wet snow), rain, long periods of high heat during summer, or a mild summer with not enough heat will affect how much you need to water your lavender plants. If the temperatures are above 90 degrees and it is windy, you will need to water more often than if you are experiencing mild temperatures and cool, still nights. Lavender will survive under snow cover, but in a dry, cold winter will appreciate being watered every four to six weeks.

If you have light, sandy soil and low rainfall, you will water more frequently than if you have clay soil. If you have sandy loam, you will water more frequently than if you have clay loam. If you have heavier soils like clay or clay loam and a lot of rainfall, you may not need to water at all except for when your lavender is newly transplanted. Mulching plants with straw, wood chips, fabric, newspaper, or gravel helps retain soil moisture, insulate plants during cold winters, and suppress unwanted weeds.

Newly transplanted plants and yearling plants (smaller plants) will need to be watered more frequently than well-established plants three years of age or older. Water sufficiently until developing flower heads are well above the uppermost leaves. When stem and flower head are fully formed, it's best to water only to avoid stress damage and loss of flowers until harvest.

Irrigation Methods

Drip irrigation deposits water directly to the roots of each plant. It requires low pressure and creates a low water flow. The benefits of using drip emitters are vast, especially in drier climates and where water is a limited resource. Water is directed to the plant only; this targeted watering means fewer weeds and conserves water by reducing evaporation. Drip irrigation is as useful in a small garden setting as in a larger application when you have multiple plants.

Your soil type dictates which emitter flow rate (gallons/liters per hour) you should choose, with a slow flow used for heavier types of soils and a faster flow for sandy soils or high-porosity soils. On our clay loam I use slow-rate emitters, allowing enough water to give a deep soak but not to flood the soil surface.

Overhead watering is not recommended for lavender. Water from overhead can damage flowers, curve stems, and affect harvesting for essential oil. If you must use it, avoid watering when flowers are blooming or close to cutting.

above and right: Anchor drip lines or emitter tubing at each end. Lines can move as much as 2 feet with changing day and night temperatures.

top: Punch a hole in ½-inch emitter tubing for each drip emitter.

center and bottom: Pop each drip emitter into a prepunched hole.

Fertilizing Your Lavender

Plants require several kinds of nutrients to thrive: primary nutrients, secondary nutrients, and trace elements. The primary nutrients are nitrogen, phosphorous, and potassium. Nitrogen is formative for plant establishment and foliage. Phosphorus is required for root development and overall plant health. Potassium is key for protecting the plant against stress, especially during long periods of varying temperatures like drought or extreme cold.

Lavender does not require lots of additional nutrients, but supplying some based on your soil type and growing conditions can be helpful. Just be mindful that nutrient requirements can vary with the seasons, and excessive amounts of fertilizer are counterproductive for lavender. Here are some general guidelines:

- Use a low-nitrogen fertilizer to aid established older plants, new lavender plantings, and potted lavender starts. For cut flowers, adding nitrogen in spring will help the plant produce more and longer stems.

- Add phosphorus right before the lavender begins to flower, to help with abundant blooms and long stems. I like to use fish emulsion as a foliar spray or a soil drench. For an immediate boost, I apply bone meal as a side dressing and water it in. Worm castings help with phosphorus intake and can be used as a side dressing or dug into your garden bed.

- Apply potassium to aid with the overall health of plants and to help protect plants going into winter so they are less likely to be injured by spring and fall frosts. Potassium also encourages strong lavender stems. Greensand is a rich source of potassium and also contains several essential trace elements, including manganese, zinc, and copper, making it an excellent choice for improving the overall health and vigor of plants.

- An application of bone meal or kelp meal around lavender plants in early fall can help make plants stronger and more winter hardy.

If your soil is lacking in nutrients, you may see these signs: the lavender plant's lower leaves turn pale yellow, the plant is not growing as expected in size and form, leaves are discolored or have spots, leaves take on a purplish-red hue during the growing season, and stems are weak. For help understanding signs of nutrient deficiency, reach out to your local extension agency or nursery.

How and When to Fertilize

IN POTS: Fertilize lavender plants growing in pots and other containers in early spring and again, if needed, in early summer. I use an organic plant food listed for use in containers or a water-soluble liquid plant food at half the recommended strength found on the product label.

IN THE GARDEN: Lavender plants growing outdoors benefit from light fertilization. This is especially true once plants are three years of age or older. Feed lightly in late winter or early spring with a mild organic plant food, such as fish emulsion, or fertilize using a shallow band of aged, composted manure alongside the row or in a circle around an individual plant. This is referred to as side dressing.

IN THE FIELD: Before planting a large area with lavender, do a soil analysis to find out if additional nutrients are necessary. The nutrient regime is different for new plants versus established plants, so do a soil analysis periodically for basic maintenance of nutrient levels. As the plant ages, lavender does not need as much fertilizer. If you are growing lavender on a larger scale and want to correct any nutrient deficiencies before plants reach their full growth potential, have plant tissue analysis done at the same place where you get your soil tested. This analysis will indicate whether your plants contain the concentrations of primary nutrients necessary for optimum growth.

Pruning Lavender

Pruning lavender stimulates new growth, removes any dead stems from the previous fall, promotes an even bloom and a prolific harvest of flowers, maintains shape, and increases lavender flower yields, especially important if you are selling your harvest. If a plant is not pruned, it gets woody in the middle and will tend to split or splay open there.

Spring is the best time to prune true lavender and lavandins, after the last hard frost. If you want plants to bloom two weeks later than they usually do, prune two weeks later than you would normally prune but before the plant begins to produce buds, or you will be removing future flowers. *Lavandula stoechas* is pruned in summer, immediately after the plant has produced its first flush of flowers. Consider a light pruning in winter followed by a heavier pruning of one-third of the plant in fall. *Lavandula dentata* generally requires little pruning unless it has

Nice tight mounds of semi-dormant *Lavandula angustifolia* 'Maillette' in springtime demonstrate that these plants have been pruned every year.

grown into a hedge. Then you can maintain the hedge shape by pruning during the summer months. Frost-tender lavenders, such as *L. pterostoechas*, may require an occasional light pruning.

In USDA zones 7 and above, you can delay pruning to fall; then no pruning is necessary in spring. Pruning in late summer and early fall promotes the formation of new flower buds and stimulates an additional bloom. This also happens if you harvest only the flowers (I call this harvesting high, or cutting high up the stem) for making essential oil. Fall pruning is an opportunity to go back and clean up the plant by removing the stems that were left after harvesting high.

When pruning *Lavandula angustifolia*, *L. ×intermedia*, and *L. stoechas* cultivars, you'll want to remove a third of the plant (up to half of the plant for *L. stoechas*) or leave three leaf nodes above the base wood of the plant. It's important not to remove more than that; otherwise the stems will die. Remove both the top and sides of the plant to maintain its shape.

When you have only a few plants or plants that are smaller in size, you can use a hand sickle to remove dead flowers. Handheld pruning shears can be used on one- to two-year-old plants. Gas or electric hedge trimmers are great to use on larger, more established plants. If you are a larger-scale or commercial grower, you can use a green tea harvester or mechanical harvester, a versatile piece of equipment that can serve not only as a hedger but also as a harvester.

At our farm, we prune more than nineteen thousand plants. We hedge back a third of the plant, or if the plants are small, we trim down to three to four leaf nodes above the base or wood. For one- to two-year-old plants, we use handheld pruning shears; for large plants, we use a hedge-trimming device.

above left and right: Pruning a first-year lavandin plant in spring, removing one-third of the plant.

Pruning a third-year true lavender plant using handheld pruners.

A pruned fourth-year plant with green tips showing it has broken dormancy.

INSIDER tip

Pruning can easily spread disease (especially sap-borne diseases like alfalfa mosaic virus), so be sure to disinfect your tools before you start pruning. Use isopropyl alcohol on a cloth to wipe your blades, or spray it on. If you identify an infected plant, skip the plant or disinfect your tools in between plants.

Using a hedger to prune a well-established lavender plant, removing one-third of the plant.

Is It Dormant—or Dead?

Every year, customers who come to my greenhouse to buy lavender in spring ask if they should remove a plant in their garden because it looks dead. My answer is, give the plant enough time to surprise you before pulling it from the ground. Lavender of all kinds but especially true lavender is slow to come out of winter dormancy, the state in which the plant exhibits little or no growth. Dormancy is a rest period when most, if not all, metabolic activity ceases. In the high desert where my farm is located, we often don't see lavender plants coming back to life until May. This is right around the time lilacs bloom.

Many times, a plant coming out of winter looks dry and brittle and may appear to be dead, but most of the time it isn't. Be patient! Your plant is beginning to wake up after being dormant. A few key indicators signal that a plant is still alive. One is new green growth from the base of the plant. Another is a light green center in a branch you break off; a dead stem will be brown and have a small pinpoint of black at its center. A third indicator is swelling growth nodes along the woody stem.

After a plant has broken dormancy and has begun to grow, you may see some winter dieback, where the plant is partially dead, perhaps on one side of the shrub. You can prune out the dead portion of the shrub and then reshape the plant. Sometimes more wood is dead than alive, and this is when I start over. I pull the plant out completely, roots and all, and plant a new lavender start.

If you see green growth coming from the base of a plant, it is still alive.

Seeing a green center inside a broken-off stem tells you the plant is still alive.

Dealing with Pests and Diseases

Being mindful of pests and diseases and practicing prevention can go a long way toward keeping lavender healthy in your garden or field. Plants stressed by climatic conditions and nutrient deficiencies are more susceptible to pests and diseases. Poor drainage facilitates fungal disease and spread, as does using equipment such as pruners, hedge trimmers, and cutters on infected plants without disinfecting them afterward.

INSECT PESTS

In a garden setting, lavender is not seriously affected by pests. For one thing, lavender is not tasty to our furry friends like rabbits and deer. On occasion they are known to pull freshly planted or young plants out, but they quickly realize they do not like the taste of the plant and leave it alone. However, when lavender is grown in a commercial environment, pests can have a significant impact on plant health and harvest if left untreated. The most common pests that cause leaf or plant damage are aphids, spittlebugs, and grasshoppers.

Aphids (*Aphis* spp.) can transmit alfalfa mosaic virus, so they should be controlled with predatory insects or an insecticide. On our farm we have planted hedgerows of wildflowers and herbs that work as a natural insecary to promote predatory and pollinator insects such as minute pirate bugs, soldier beetles, and hoverflies. If you have to resort to an insecticide, use one that will not affect all the pollinators and is bee friendly, such as an insecticidal soap based on potassium salts of naturally derived fatty acids, or one that targets soft-bodied insects. Another option is releasing aphid parasites like the parasitoid wasp *Aphelinus abdominalis*.

Spittlebugs or froghoppers (*Philaenus spumarius*) can be found on lavender in early summer in some parts of the world. They are known for frothy foam they produce while feeding on plants. Their presence typically causes little damage, though if populations are high, stems can be slightly deformed. To prevent them from overwintering in your garden, remove weeds and fall leaves where adults lay eggs. If you find them on your plants, you can physically remove them by hand or spray them with a strong blast of water to dislodge nymphs, which will prevent them from returning.

Grasshoppers (suborder Caelifera) can be more present in drought years and warm, dry springs. A large enough grasshopper population can cause considerable damage. They are known to nibble the stems of lavender just enough to cause the flower to wilt, so if you want to harvest your flowers before they are spent, do not delay. As prevention, grow a border of a trap crop like grass that will keep them busy. Set out bird feeders around your garden to attract birds, and/or raise chickens or guinea hens, all natural predators. My first inspiration to get chickens on my farm was the grasshoppers, a delicacy to my feathered friends. Other natural predators are wasps, ground beetles, robber flies, and parasitoids such as horsehair worms and tachinid flies. You can also buy a bait made from wheat bran flakes coated with *Nosema locustae*, a disease organism that when ingested kills grasshoppers.

FUNGAL AND BACTERIAL DISEASES

The main fungal and bacterial diseases that can infect lavender are yellow decline, alfalfa mosaic virus, and phytophthora root and crown rot.

Yellow decline comes from *Stolbur phytoplasma*, a bacterium spread by leafhoppers, and causes early decline of a lavender plant. As prevention, practice good hygiene and plant resistant species and cultivars.

Alfalfa mosaic virus occurs in many wild and ornamental plants. Symptoms include a bright yellow mosaic pattern causing leaves to molt. The virus is transmitted by aphids or cutting tools. There is no cure, unfortunately, and infected plants need to be removed and destroyed. If plants are not removed the infection will spread.

Alfalfa mosaic virus's distinctive yellow pattern is starting to show on these plants.

To prevent alfalfa mosaic virus, practice good hygiene, clean your tools, and remove and burn infected plants. Stressed and undernourished plants can be vulnerable to viruses, so make sure to fertilize and water when needed. Plant an insectary hedgerow to promote predatory insects like ladybirds (lady bugs), hoverflies, lacewings, and parasitic wasps that prey on aphids.

Phytophthora root and crown rot affects the most common species of lavender and can be very damaging. The disease normally begins as the wilt and browning of a few branches of an individual plant. As the disease progresses, more of the plant wilts, and eventually the whole plant dies. Neighboring plants will often begin to show symptoms of the disease as the pathogen slowly moves through the soil. The most common phytophthora affecting lavender, *Phytophthora nicotianae*, will destroy new plants within a week or two under very moist conditions and can then spread down the row to neighboring fields and be washed downhill to low areas.

Signs of phytophthora in *Lavandula angustifolia* include dieback in the middle of the plant, spreading to other parts of the plant and to neighboring plants.

Phytophthoras belong to a group of fungal-like organisms called Oomycetes, or water molds. They produce spore sacs called sporangia that release numerous swimming zoospores. Many species of *Phytophthora*, including the ones that attack lavender, naturally live in soil. The disease requires very moist conditions to flourish in lavender fields and can be present in the soil for years before showing up. It can also be introduced by planting contaminated transplants, plants dug up in a contaminated area and moved to a new location. Once an infected plant is placed in your garden or field, it becomes the source from which the pathogen can become established in your soil and spread to other plants.

Buy plants from a reputable nursery to avoid planting diseased plants in the first place. Plants with symptoms should be removed immediately, along with the surrounding soil, and healthy plants on either side should also be removed. The garden or field should then be continuously monitored for further disease spread. Avoid planting lavender back into the same spot, as the pathogen may still remain in the soil; instead, consider planting nonhost ornamentals. If you plan to plant lots of lavender, test your soil for *Phytophthora* species first and avoid planting where pathogens are present. Strains vary depending on where you are; the ones that are detrimental to lavender are *P. nicotianae* (the most common), *P. palmivora*, *P. cinnamomi*, and *P. cactorum*.

Weed Control

In any garden, weeds are ever-present. The challenge is not to eliminate them completely but to minimize them. Farming and growing organically eliminates herbicides as an option—one less tool in the toolbox—but I have found numerous other creative ways to suppress weeds over the years. The most effective methods I have found are cover cropping and woven fabric. As the plant is first developing, hand weeding around the plant works best. As the lavender plants grow larger, the plants themselves crowd out the weeds. Which weed control method you decide to use will depend on whether you have lavender planted in a garden setting or a lavender patch.

HAND-WEEDING TOOLS

We use all kinds of hand-weeding tools plus a stirrup hoe to control the weeds around plants. The blade of the stirrup hoe works beneath the soil surface to cut weeds at the root with a back-and-forth motion. It allows you to remove weeds in tight places between rows and plants. Every season I replace my weeding hoe blades because they get a lot of use and are worn down quickly by all the rocks in the soil. These rocks make for great drainage for the lavender plants but are not so great for my hoe blades.

FABRIC MULCH

To squelch weeds in larger spaces, we use water-permeable woven polypropylene fabric in the furrows and garden beds. This is an herbicide-free way to prevent weeds from putting down deep roots around cultivated plants and landscaping. The fabric is treated to withstand UV rays and perfect for aboveground applications; it can also be used in the ground for soil stabilization. Heavier-weight fabric, from 3.1-ounce to 5-ounce, is longer-lasting and suitable for lavender. Natural mulch such as rock, paper, and bark can also be very effective. Paper mulch naturally biodegrades and can be tilled back into the soil.

MECHANICAL CULTIVATION (TILLAGE)

Tillage is a process that involves using small equipment like a rototiller or some type of mechanical implement pulled by a tractor to slice, chop, or uproot small weeds. This mechanical cultivation can be very effective when you are growing lavender on a large scale. It saves time and requires less labor than weeding by hand.

COVER CROPPING

Cover cropping is a mainstay on our farm. Cover crops are plants grown primarily to protect and enhance the soil and to benefit future crops. Cover cropping can not only help suppress weeds by crowding out weed seedlings but also add organic matter and nutrients to the soil. Cover crops can also be planted in a garden.

    Before planting any new field of lavender, I plant a winter or spring cover crop. My winter cover is generally winter rye because it does not need to be irrigated and relies on natural winter and spring moisture. For a spring cover crop, I like to seed a grass, legume, and brassica

INSIDER tip

The right cover crop for your garden or farm depends on your climate, soil, and objectives. Resources to help you decide on the right cover crop are available through your local agricultural extension. You can locate seed suppliers online.

132   LAVENDER FOR ALL SEASONS

rapa mix. This includes sudan grass, oats, turnips, vetch, and sweet peas. If I plan to plant the field in lavender the same season, I till the cover crop. Otherwise, I mow the cover crop so I can reseed the area or let the cover crop come back on its own.

Protecting Lavender in Cold and Adverse Conditions

There are a few simple things you can do to increase the chances of your lavender plants surviving extreme temperatures without tissue damage and winter kill.

True lavender and lavandin plants go dormant in winter, but they still depend on a bit of moisture to sustain them through their dormancy. And while snowy winters can provide enough moisture and insulation to keep lavender plants happy and healthy, in dry winters without snow cover or rain, they're going to need a little help. If there has been little to no snow cover where you live, water lavender plants deeply every four to six weeks in winter. Add mulch to help retain moisture and keep plant roots warm.

Create shelter from wind by planting a windbreak or populating surrounding beds with larger perennials like tall grasses, bushes, and evergreens that will not be as sensitive to high winds. This adds protection and also color and a diversity of texture and height in your landscape.

For more cold-sensitive lavender cultivars, you can use a floating row cover that allows light and water in but protects your plants from extreme cold. The fabric is light enough that it is not necessary to hoop it. Just stretch it out over your plants, weighting the excess fabric on either side with whatever you have on hand, like rocks or logs. Only use when winter temperatures are below 50 degrees F; otherwise plants can get too warm underneath the fabric and break dormancy too soon. Once weather warms, you should remove the fabric.

FLOATING FABRIC GRADES AND PROTECTION RATINGS

Grade	Standard	Medium	Heavy	Extra heavy
Weight per square yard	.55 oz	.9 oz	1.5 oz	2.0 oz
Frost protection (added number of degrees)	2°–4°F (1.1°–2.2°C)	4°–6°F (2.2°–3.3°C)	6°–8°F (3.3°–4.4°C)	8+°F (4.4+°C)
Light transmission	85%	70%	50%	30%

Companion Planting

Lavender naturally lends itself to being grown with other flowering perennials and aromatic herbs. I love cultivating different scents in my family cottage garden and on my farm. I find myself walking down rows of herbs and borders with my hands freely touching the plants and then smelling my fingers. I do it without even noticing! I will often pick leaves, rub them between my fingers, and hold the leaves or flower buds up to my nose, which gives me a sense of peace and harmony. Taking a moment here and there to smell the fragrant herbs growing around our farm is a true pleasure.

BLOOMING PERENNIAL COMPANIONS

Combining lavender with compatible plants that bloom at the same time creates a display of color and texture along with a feeding zone for pollinators. I enjoy wandering the garden to observe the array of pollinators and beneficial bugs, including butterflies, hummingbirds, honeybees, bumblebees, native bees, hoverflies, and praying mantises. Over the years I have discovered that these same plants can complement fresh-cut or dried lavender in a flower bouquet.

A mix of blooming perennials that have the same growing requirements: yarrow in various shades, rudbeckia, delphinium, and dianthus.

Blooming perennials that combine especially well with the hues of lavender. From left to right: yellow yarrow, red yarrow, 'Green Twister' coneflower, black-eyed Susan, sunflowers, fennel, and cardoon.

FLOWERING COMPANIONS FOR LAVENDER

Latin name	Common name	Flower colors	USDA hardiness zones	Blooms same time as
PERENNIAL FLOWERS				
Achillea spp.	yarrow	white, yellow, rust, red, pink	zones 4–7	lavandins
Agastache spp.	hummingbird mint, hyssop	pink, orange, red	zone 5	lavandins
Artemisia spp.	common wormwood	white or yellow flowers, silver foliage	zones 4–8	lavandins
Buddleja davidii	butterfly bush	white, pink, purple, maroon	zones 5–9	lavandins
Cerastium tomentosum	snow in summer	white flowers, silver foliage	zones 3–9	angustifolias
Centranthus ruber	Jupiter's beard	red, pink	zones 4–9	lavandins in summer and angustifolias in fall
Coreopsis spp.	tickseed	white, yellow, orange, red, pink	zones 2–11	angustifolias
Delphinium grandiflora	delphinium	blue, lavender, pink	zone 5	angustifolias
Echinacea spp.	coneflower	orange, bronze, red, purple, yellow, green	zones 4–9	lavandins
Echinops spp.	globe thistle	blue flowers, silver foliage	zones 3–8	lavandins
Eryngium spp.	sea holly	blue and purple flowers, silver foliage	zones 4–8	lavandins
Gaillardia spp.	blanket flower	yellow, bronze, orange, red	zones 3–8	angustifolias
Kniphofia spp.	red hot poker	red, orange, yellow	zones 5–10	lavandins
Monarda didyma	crimson bee balm	red, wine red, pink	zones 4–8	lavandins
Papaver orientale	Oriental poppy	white, orange, pink, red	zones 3–7	angustifolias
Penstemon spp.	beardtongue	red, orange, pink, blue, yellow	zones 3–8	angustifolias and lavandins
Ratibida Columnifera	prairie coneflower, Mexican hat	orange, yellow, bronze, red	zones 4–8	lavandins
Rudbeckia spp.	black-eyed Susan	yellow, bronze, orange	zones 3–9	lavandins
Salvia greggii	autumn sage	white, peach, orange, pink, violet, red	zones 6–9	angustifolias
Salvia officinalis	garden sage	purple flowers, silver foliage	zones 4–10	angustifolias and lavandins
Salvia ×sylvestris	wood sage	purple-blue	zones 4–8	angustifolias
Sedum spp.	stonecrop	red, pink, yellow	zones 4–9	angustifolias and lavandins
Stachys byzantina	lamb's ear	pink to purple flowers, silver foliage	zones 4–8	angustifolias

Latin name	Common name	Flower colors	USDA hardiness zones	Blooms same time as
PERENNIAL SHRUBS OR VINES				
Berberis thunbergii	Japanese barberry	burgundy foliage	zones 4–8	
Eunonymus fortunei	wintercreeper	yellow-green foliage	zones 5a–9a	
Lonicera caprifolium	honeysuckle	yellow, red, orange	zones 5–9	
ANNUAL FLOWERS (ALL WILL SELF-SEED ONCE ESTABLISHED)				
Amaranthus cruentus	amaranth	red, bronze		lavandins
Ammi majus	bishop's weed, Queen Anne's lace	white, burgundy		lavandins
Calendula spp.	calendula	orange, yellow		angustifolia and lavandins
Centaurea cyanus	cornflower, bachelor's button	blue, pale blue, pink, maroon		angustifolia and lavandins
Cosmos spp.	cosmos	red, pink, white		angustifolia and lavandins
Helianthus annuus	sunflower	yellow, bronze, green, orange, white		lavandins
Papaver rhoeas	corn poppy, Shirley poppy	red, pink	zones 4–9	lavandins
Zinnia elegans	zinnia	white, yellow, orange, red, pink, violet, green		lavandins

Helicrysum italica and *papaver rhoeas* (in the background), planted among lavender.

TEA GARDEN INSPIRATIONS

Teatime, anyone? Lavender is a wonderful complement to tea herbs such as lemon balm, lemon verbena, chamomile, and mint. These herbs not only go together in tea but also grow well together. You can combine lavender with herbs to either calm or energize you in a fresh or a dried tea blend. A planting area of calming scents and tea blends can include true lavender, hyssop, chamomile, and wild bergamot. *Lavandula angustifolia* cultivars I like to use in tea are 'Buena Vista', 'Croxton's Wild', and 'Folgate'.

I feel exhilarated when I pick thyme or mint, so these belong in an area of energizing scents and tea blends. Try including a mild lavandin, rosemary, lemon balm, and different mints in this area. Some of my favorites are peppermint, pineapple mint, mountain mint, orange mint, and double mint. Try planting mints for tea in different-size containers or planters. If you are in USDA zone 5 or lower, consider bringing the cold-sensitive plants indoors during winter. In spring, scatter those pots throughout your planting area for a theme garden.

This herb garden features raised beds that include 'Gardenview Scarlet' bee balm, bergamot, and chives, surrounded by *Lavandula angustifolia* 'Imperial Gem'.

TEA GARDEN COMPANIONS FOR LAVENDER

Latin name	Common name	USDA hardiness zones	Garden notes
Agastache foeniculum	anise hyssop	zones 4–9	Harvest and dry leaves for tea.
Agastache rugosa	Korean mint	zones 7–9	Can grow in partial shade. Licorice scent. Use young leaves in salad and teas.
Agastache scrophulariifolia	purple giant hyssop	zones 4–9	Can grow in partial shade. Leaves are edible, so use in salads and teas.
Aloysia citrodora	lemon verbena	zones 8–9	In colder zones, keep in a pot and bring in during cold months. Brew tea with dried or fresh leaves.
Chamaemelum nobile	Roman chamomile	zones 5–9	Low growing, so can be used as an aromatic ground cover. Makes an apple-scented tea.
Hibiscus sabdariffa	roselle	zones 9–12	In zones below 8, grow as 110-day summer annual. Start early and harvest fruity calyxes before first frost.
Ilex paraguariensis	yerba mate	zones 9–12	Grows well in a container under a covered patio or in a greenhouse. I grow this herb in my greenhouse and enjoy blending it with lavender buds, lemon verbena, and dried tea leaves.
Matricaria recutita	German chamomile	zones 5–9	Withstands frost. Let reseed in zones 1–6. Has upright growth.
Melissa officinalis	lemon balm	zones 5–9	Versatile herb with citrusy flavor and mild lemon aroma. Blends well with other herbs.
Mentha ×piperita	peppermint	zones 5–9	Keep all mints in a dedicated mint bed or in pots to prevent unwanted spread in your garden.
Mentha spicata	spearmint	zones 3–7	Much milder than peppermint. Wonderful with honey and lemon.
Mentha suaveolens	pineapple mint or apple mint	zones 4–9	Mild fruity and minty flavor balances other tea herbs.
Monarda citriodora	lemon balm, lemon bergamot	zones 4–9	Use leaves and purple flowers to add lemon flavor to cooked foods, salads, and teas. To enjoy flowers throughout summer, deadhead flowers. Grow monardas in moisture-retentive and loamy soil high in organic matter.
Monarda didyma	crimson or scarlet beebalm, Oswego tea	zones 4–8	Add red flower to salads. For a relaxing tea, combine with chamomile and lavender.
Monarda fistulosa	wild bergamot	zones 3–10	Lavender-pink edible flowers. Has a spicy flavor similar to oregano and thyme and makes a great substitute for those herbs. Enhances teas.
Nepeta cataria	catnip	zones 4–9	Combine with chamomile and lavender for a soothing bedtime tea.
Ocimum ×citriodorum	Mrs. Burns lemon basil	zones 7–9	Grow like you would any basil. Lasts longer in hot climates if grown in partial shade. Use fresh or dried.
Ocimum tenuiflorum	holy basil, tulsi	zones 10–12	In zones below 10, grow in pots or keep as an annual in your garden.

KITCHEN HERB GARDEN INSPIRATIONS

I love having an herb garden that is accessible from my kitchen so that I can just dash out for herbs when I'm in the middle of cooking. Aromatic herbs to consider that marry well with buds of true lavender in savory dishes are basil, coriander, dill, fennel, marjoram, oregano, rosemary, sage, savory, and thyme. I plant these herbs not only in my garden beds but also in pots on my patio where I can quickly trim what I need for fresh seasonings that will complement weeknight meals.

Note that although the herbs in the table pair well with lavender, not all have the same cultural requirements. Basil, chervil, fennel, and marjoram need more water than lavender, so plant apart. Summer savory, winter savory, lemon thyme, and thyme can all be combined with lavender in a perennial herb bed.

A kitchen garden with potted lavender, variegated sage, thyme, and rosemary.

KITCHEN HERB COMPANIONS FOR LAVENDER

Latin name	Common name	USDA hardiness zones	Garden notes
Angelica archangelica	angelica	zones 4–9	
Anthriscus cerefolium	chervil	zones 7–9	Withstands mild frost. In zone 6 and below, treat as an annual or let reseed.
Foeniculum vulgare	fennel	zones 7–9	Open-pollinated cultivars will self-seed.
Lippia graveolens	Mexican oregano	zones 10–11	In zone 9 and below, treat as a summer annual.
Ocimum basilicum	basil, sweet basil	zones 9–11	In zone 8 and below, treat as a summer annual.
Origanum heracleoticum	Greek oregano	zones 5–9	Will spread and can make a nice ground cover.
Origanum majorana	sweet marjoram	zones 8–12	
Origanum syriacum	Syrian oregano, za'atar	zones 8–12	
Rosmarinus officinalis	rosemary	zones 6–11	Hardiness depends on cultivar.
Salvia officinalis	common sage	zones 5–9	Same growing requirements as lavender. Dries beautifully and complements lavender in flavor and ornamental bouquets.
Satureja hortensis	summer savory	zones 6–9	Same growing requirements as lavender.
Satureja montana	winter savory	zones 5–9	Same growing requirements as lavender.
Thymus ×citriodorus	lemon thyme	zones 6–9	Can be used in teas as well. Same growing requirements as lavender.
Thymus vulgaris	thyme	zones 5–9	Same growing requirements as lavender.

Chapter 4

The Lavender Harvest

Once summertime has arrived, waking up early comes naturally. The anticipation of the morning harvest always gets me out of bed. Even with the pressure of all the chores that need to be done later in the day, spending a few hours cutting fresh flowers in the cool dawn is always calming and clears my mind. The existential questions about my farming endeavors (it's not always easy!) that sometimes visit me in wintertime seem to disappear, and I feel a true sense of rejuvenation.

It is during summer as we prepare to harvest our lavender flowers that all our efforts come full circle: the propagating, the planting, the watering, the pruning. The landscape I have created with mother nature reverberates with the rhythm of the hand sickle cutting through the stems in one swift movement. I bundle the fresh-cut stems with the rubber bands around my wrist and place the bundles on top of the now-rounded shrubs so they stay clean and are visible when gathering time arrives. The lavender summer harvest has begun.

When you have enjoyed the lingering notes of purple, pink, and violet lent by lavender to your garden landscape, it is time to harvest your flowers. For most growing zones, harvest will begin in late spring or early summer. If you choose to cut your flowers, a few handling tips will give you pleasing results and help you enjoy lavender beyond just this one season. Earlier in the book, I indicated which cultivars have desirable attributes for crafting, specifically referencing stem length, color, and form. In this chapter I discuss when to harvest depending on what you would like to do with your stems, the tools and materials you will need in order to harvest and handle cut lavender, how to handle your bundles, and the most effective ways to remove the buds from the stems.

When Do I Cut My Flowers?

The timing of your lavender harvest makes all the difference in how your crafting endeavors turn out. Every stem on a lavender shrub does not bloom at exactly the same time. Stems vary in how many flowers or corollas are open, closed, or withered. Lavender flowers picked too early will droop, and when they are dried, no flower will be visible and you will end up with just a skinny twig. Lavender picked too late will often have no color, with faded or brown corollas remaining on the stem.

The dried wreaths and bouquets we offer from our farm are so colorful that visitors often think we treat our flowers with a preservative, or they think they are admiring fresh flowers. This is all about the timing of harvest. The time of day you cut your flowers, how open the flower buds are on their spike, and how the bundles are dried, as well as the specific lavender cultivar you're growing, all make a difference. I have learned tricks over the years that can vastly improve the quality of flower bouquets, potpourri, and essential oil yields.

For starters, I use a bud maturity scoring system the New Zealanders have developed that works very well. This may be too technical for some, but I find it very useful to help answer the question of when to cut my flowers. In general, you want to harvest a stem of lavender for fresh bundles when on average half of the buds are open and half are closed, which means when the bud maturity score is 3 to 5.

Here's how to score your lavender in three easy steps. As time goes on and you practice more, you will develop an eye for the different levels of bud maturity. When

above: Three different bloom stages (left to right): sprig one has maturity score 1, sprig two has maturity score 2 and sprigs three and four have maturity scores 3 and 4.

left: Begin harvesting lavender when on average half the buds are open and half are closed.

THE LAVENDER HARVEST   145

BUD MATURITY SCALE

Maturity score	Description		Harvest notes
1	Flower head has no open flowers. This is the bud stage.		Wait to harvest.
2	The first one or two flowers are open.		Wait to harvest.
3	Several flowers are open but none has withered. Many buds are still closed.		Begin harvest for fresh and dried bundles.
4	Several flowers are open, and some are beginning to wither.		Harvest for fresh and dried bundles.
5	The number of buds and withered flowers is approximately equal; some flowers are open.		Begin harvesting to process for essential oil or hydrosol.
6	A few buds are left; some flowers are open but most are withered.		Harvest for maximum yields of essential oil or hydrosol.
7	No buds remain; a few flowers are open but most are withered.		Harvest for maximum yields of essential oil or hydrosol.
8	All flowers are withered.		Harvest for essential oil or hydrosol.
8+	Capsules are starting to open and shed seed.		

you are beginning and have lots to harvest, you can "run the numbers" to see if your plants are ready to harvest.

1. Take a sample of fifty stems from a random area of your lavender planting.

2. Assign a number score to each stem.

3. Add all the scores and divide by fifty to calculate the average score for the sample. The score will indicate the overall bud development stage of your planting.

Variability between flowers is unavoidable, and that is where your overall average score can help. One or two stems may not be ready, but the rest of your stems will be.

As far as time of day, harvesting in the early morning before the heat arrives is best. In the heat of the day, essential oils can volatize. If you harvest in the cool of the morning, the lavender will hold more oil. Your fresh bundles will retain their aroma longer, and if you are distilling your flower stems, your yields will be higher.

Harvesting for Bouquets and Essential Oil

When harvest time arrives, gather these materials:

- good-quality rubber bands, size #33 (3½ × ⅛ inch)
- hand sickle or hand pruner
- basket
- bucket
- pencil and paper to label what type of lavender and the date you cut your flowers

HARVESTING FOR DRIED BUNDLES

You can harvest with a hand pruner or a hand sickle, but harvesting using a hand sickle is a time saver as it allows you to cut multiple stems at once. It's also easier on your wrist. Be mindful where your fingers are—tuck them inward. Cut low so that you get long stems, but don't cut into the woody base of the plant. Cutting into the wood can damage and ruin the form of your plant.

Bundle with good-quality rubber bands, wrapping a rubber band three times around each bundle of stems. It is disappointing when you hang your bundle to dry and then find it shattered on the floor or loose all over the ground because of a weak rubber band.

If you are cutting many bundles at a time, place the finished bundles on top of shrubs to make sure you do not lose track of them and to keep them clean. Remember a single mature plant can produce upward of nine to twelve bundles per plant.

You can label your bundles in the garden or field with type of lavender and date if you are harvesting many different types of lavender. On our farm, we gather the bundles separately by cultivar to transport them to the drying room and then label each drying rack with the field, the cultivar name, and the date harvested. This way, I can keep track of how much time the bundles are taking to dry.

Wrap a rubber band three times around each bundle.

HARVESTING FOR FRESH-CUT BOUQUETS

For fresh-cut bouquets, have a bucket filled with about 2 inches of water ready before you begin harvesting. Cut and bundle your lavender flowers as you would for drying and then place the stems in the water. Change out the water daily to prevent the flowers from turning brown and the stems from getting slimy and slick. Fresh-cut bouquets will last five to seven days, especially if you keep them in a cool place or store them in a refrigerator at 34 degrees F (1 degree C). After you have enjoyed a fresh-cut lavender bouquet in a vase of water for about four days, you can then dry the bouquet and enjoy it year-round!

HARVESTING FOR ESSENTIAL OIL

Whether you are harvesting lavender for home distilling or for distilling on a large scale, the same principles apply. The level of essential oils in the lavender flowers is highest when the flowers are 50 to 100 percent open. In other words, when the overall bud maturity scores are between 5 and 8 is the optimum time to harvest for essential oil distillation.

Harvest lavender for essential oil when the flowers are 50 to 100 percent open.

I prefer to distill only fresh plant material rather than dry material because the oil yields tend to be higher and the levels of compounds more favorable. Since most of the chemical compounds are in the calyx, I harvest high—meaning I cut the flowers close to the top of the plant, leaving most of the stem and taking the spikes. On a small scale like a garden or small farm, a hand sickle works fine; on a small or medium-size farm, use a green tea harvester; on a large farm, use a combine.

If you are harvesting by hand, there is no need to bundle the stems, so you can harvest loose material into a basket or tub. This also allows you to fit more of the plant material into the still. You can let the plant material sit for up to twelve hours before distilling, preferably spread out on a tarp or concrete slab if there's a lot of it. If you do let a large quantity of harvested flowers sit—or "cure"—make sure you turn the material every two hours with a pitchfork so it does not get hot or begin to mold.

When cutting flowers for essential oil, harvest high—near the top of the plant—and gather the loose material in a basket or tub.

Drying Lavender Bundles

What you are aiming for in a dried lavender bundle is one that maintains its color and shape for a long time, does not shatter, and is aromatic. Picking your flowers at the proper stage of bloom makes a significant difference, as does having a drying area with plenty of space to suspend bundles upside down, with good air circulation and little to no light. Suspending bundles upside down will result in nice straight stems and full bundles. Whether you are drying one bundle or hundreds, you need a dark, dry place such as a pantry, an attic, a basement, or a shed.

Have these materials on hand to hang your freshly harvested bundles to dry:

- a grade 30 or 43 cargo chain for hanging a pillar of bundles OR
- a long string or wire for hanging bundles clothesline-style OR
- wire fencing with a 6-by-8-inch rectangular grid, sometimes referred to as hog wire fencing
- heavy-duty steel screw hooks measuring at least 4½ inches long
- large plastic-coated paper clips or wire cut to 6 inches long and shaped into an S for hooks
- a humidifier for dry climates or conditions
- an oscillating or box fan for humid climates or conditions

You will hang each bundle by hooking it to something that will suspend it in the air while it dries. A chain fastened to the ceiling or beams in a basement or barn and then covered with bundles of drying lavender hooked to it can be visually stunning—a pillar of lavender. You can also hang bundles from a long piece of string or wire suspended horizontally clothesline-style. For hanging a large number of bundles, wire fencing with a 6-by-8-inch rectangular grid hung vertically from a ceiling or beam with heavy-duty screw hooks works well. If you suspend the wire fencing so both sides are accessible, you can hang a lot more bundles.

To prepare a freshly harvested bundle for hanging, make a hook by opening a large plastic-coated paper clip or using a 6-inch length of wire to form an S shape and then secure this hook to the bundle by slipping the lower part of the S under the rubber band. Alternatively, I find I can hang bundles quickly if I first secure the hook to whatever I am going to suspend the lavender from and then hang each bundle by slipping the lower part of the S under the rubber band on the bundle.

The level of humidity in your area will affect your drying times greatly. In dry climates or conditions, you will find the bundles dry quickly in less than a week. If your area is extremely dry, you can add humidity to a room with a humidifier to prevent the bundles from losing their aroma and becoming brittle while drying. I find the ideal humidity level to be between 20 and 50 percent, lower for more humid climates and higher for dry climates. In humid climates or conditions, you will want to ensure the air is circulating by setting up an oscillating or box fan in the room

Lavender bundles hung from wire fencing to dry.

or pantry where you are drying your bundles. Maintaining good air circulation will prevent the bundles from molding and help them dry more quickly.

To prevent mold from growing in the center of a bundle, make sure it is completely dry before removing it from the drying rack. Many times, a bundle can appear dry from the outside, but the inside can feel damp or fresh. Because the center of the bundle dries last, making your bundles a bit smaller will allow them to dry more quickly. To check if a bundle is all the way dry, remove the bundle from its drying hook, remove the rubber band, and spread the stems to expose the center of the bundle. I often do a random check of my bundles throughout the drying area to see if they are completely dry.

Once the bundles are dried, remove them from your hanging system in order to ensure that they last, keeping their color and holding their flowers. If you are not going to use them right away, store them in a box—cardboard, wooden, or plastic, whatever you have on hand—either upright or sideways. You can store them sleeved in a floral sleeve or wrap each bundle in paper, like tissue or kraft paper.

Dried bundles of *Lavandula* ×*intermedia* 'Impress Purple' wrapped in kraft paper for sale.

THE LAVENDER HARVEST 153

Stripping and Cleaning Dried Lavender

Once the lavender bundles have dried, you can remove the buds from the stems to use in crafting projects or cooking. A number of different debudding methods will work, depending on the scale of your operation.

One quick and easy method involves stripping the buds from the stems by hand. Simply wrap the dried bundle in a clean flour-sack dish towel or in tissue paper and roll it like a rolling pin until all the dried buds have been released. The buds will have dust, stems, bracts, and leaves mixed in, so you will want to clean them.

I like to use three screens to clean my lavender buds. I start with a larger gauge to filter out large stems and leaves while letting the buds fall through. Then I use a smaller gauge to retain the buds and let small bracts, dust, more leaves, and calyxes fall through. Finally, I use an even finer screen to remove the fine dust and dirt particles. You can make your own screens or use fine-mesh stainless steel colanders to clean your lavender buds.

To scale up the stripping process, I use a chimney brush attached to a variable-speed drill. This assembly sits atop a barrel that collects the stripped buds.

If you need to clean hundreds of pounds of lavender, a seed cleaner of the same type you would use to clean grass seed works best. When I first started cleaning buds at a considerable volume, I decided to have a seed cleaner from the 1940s refurbished, one that a friend of mine found in an old barn in the midwestern United States. As my farm's lavender planting grew, I upgraded to a more modern version that uses the same technology and yields a higher quantity of cleaned buds. There are also off-market combination debudders and bud cleaners made specifically for lavender. Volume per hour can vary from 5 to 50 pounds per hour, depending on the type of machinery.

A quick and easy debudding method is wrapping and rolling a dried bundle.

INSIDER tip

To determine the mesh size of a screen, start from the center of one wire and count the number of openings to a point exactly one linear inch away. For example, a 4-mesh screen has four openings in one linear inch. The larger the number of openings, the smaller the mesh and the smaller the particles it will filter out. Use stainless steel mesh if you are cleaning buds for culinary use.

I use three gauges of screens to clean lavender buds.

Before and after stripping the buds from a dried bundle using a chimney brush attached to a variable-speed drill.

A grass and grain seed cleaner from the 1940s.

Scoops of lavender buds before and after cleaning with a seed cleaner.

A side-by-side comparison of chaff—small bracts, dust, stems, leaves, and tiny corollas—on the left alongside cleaned buds on the right.

Stems left over from debudding, great for garden mulch or bundled for fire starters or smudge sticks.

Make use of discarded lavender stems. In my garden and lavender bed furrows, I mulch with fresh or dried lavender stems and the leftover stems from my still. They form a lasting mulch that discourages weeds and provides a thick layer of organic matter to walk on between the rows of plants.

To maintain freshness and color, store buds in a plastic tote container in a cool, dry place until you are ready to use them.

Summer days on my farm begin and end with stillness. During the quiet hours at the end of the day when everyone has gone home or my family is off doing their summer activities, lavender bundles are suspended from makeshift devices and the still's gas burner radiates heat on an already-warm day. The perfume of sweet earth and grass fills the air as droplets of essential oil are being carried through the condenser. I am bathed in the aromas of lavender as I record my distillation notes in my binder: start times, end times, ambient conditions of the day, whether dry or humid, mild or exceptionally hot. All these factors will affect the outcome of my distillation. As the sun lowers to the west, I put away jars filled with distillate and essential oil and check hanging lavender bundles for dryness. The day's work is complete, and I am left with creations to share throughout the seasons.

Eighteen Fragrant Uses for Dried Lavender Buds

Here are some ideas I have collected over the years about how to use dried lavender buds in crafting projects. One bundle of dried lavandin will produce one cup of dried buds. The yield from true lavender is harder to estimate, as there is so much variation in buds and whorls on the stem.

FOR THE MIND/BODY

- **BATH OR FOOT SCRUB:** Mix dried buds with salts, essential oil, sugar, honey, and your favorite carrier oil.
- **BATH SOAK:** Fill a large sealable tea bag or muslin tea bag with dried buds and throw it in your tub for a relaxing soak.
- **HERBAL TINCTURE:** Make an herbal tincture by steeping dried buds in high-proof alcohol like vodka over a long period of time. Add the tincture to your favorite unscented lotion or add a few drops to water or tea.
- **SOAP:** If you make soap, add dried lavender buds to scent the soap and act as an exfoliant.

FOR THE HOME

- **CHICKEN COOP:** Placing dried buds in chickens' nesting boxes will keep them healthy. The lavender relaxes the chickens and helps prevent mites at the same time.
- **SACHETS:** Sew or buy simple sachet bags and stuff them with dried buds. Use sachets in the car, in drawers, in the linen closet, and looped over clothes hangers in the closet to help prevent moths and scent your clothes and linens at the same time.
- **DRYER BAGS:** Place dried buds in a linen bag or a large sealable tea bag and place in the dryer with your sheets.
- **CARPET DEODORIZER:** Sprinkle dried buds on your carpet and vacuum them up.
- **BATHROOM DEODORIZER:** Fill a bowl with lavender buds and place it in the bathroom.
- **PENCIL HOLDER:** Improve your well-being while working at your desk. Fill a clear vase halfway with lavender buds and stick your favorite pens and pencils in it.
- **CANDLE ACCENT:** Fill a votive candleholder partway with dried buds and nestle a votive candle in the buds.

Clean, dry lavandin buds ready to use for filling hand-painted sachets. One bundle of lavandin yielded one cup of buds.

FOR SPECIAL OCCASIONS

- **WEDDING TOSS:** Instead of rice, toss lavender buds as the couple exits the wedding ceremony. Make paper cones for the buds to hand out to guests and on the outside stamp "Kiss, Cheers, Toss."
- **SACHET BOWL:** As a party favor, set out a "Make your own sachet" project. Fill a large bowl with dried buds and provide a spoon or scoop and empty fabric sachet bags that guests can fill with buds to take home.
- **GREETING CARD CONFETTI:** Surprise!

IF YOU'RE A SEAMSTRESS

- **NECK WRAP:** Make a large rectangular bag out of flannel or chenille and fill it with flaxseed and dried lavender buds. Microwave to heat it up.
- **LAVENDER-SCENTED STUFFED TOY OR ANIMAL:** Sew a lavender sachet into your child's favorite stuffed toy or make a stuffed animal filled with lavender buds.
- **MUG COASTER:** Fill a small square fabric pouch with enough dried lavender buds to make a quarter-inch layer when the pouch is flat, and park your hot beverage on it. The heat will release the calming aroma.
- **THROW PILLOW:** Fill a throw pillow with dried lavender buds to scent your bedroom or living room.

Chicken coop freshened up with lavender buds.

Chapter 5

Growing Lavender on a Larger Scale

Every spring, customers come to the farm to pick up their preordered plants. They are excited and eager to realize their dream of a lavender farm, a lavender patch, or a lavender garden. They often ask basic questions about how to begin scaling up. I always want to make sure every gardener and farmer is set up for success, so I have thought a lot about how to narrow my answers down to a few basic concepts that produce successful results. This chapter tells what I know. It specifically addresses the potential hobby or commercial farmer, or the gardener who wants to remove lawn and replace it with lavender.

Whether your design is for a 100-square-foot plot or a square acre, the approach is the same. First, consider the end goals of your design. Will your lavender planting be used for agritourism, large production, a market garden, or an apothecary garden, such as a mixed herbal garden? Second, choose your plant species and cultivars based on growing zone and personal or business ambitions. Third, define exactly how you would like to use your bounty, which may involve considering the potential market for your lavender crop. Fourth, know your soil, as this will determine how you will prepare your growing space. Fifth, do the math to determine how many plants you will need and determine which materials and equipment you will require. Then learn to propagate lavender so you will be able to supply as many plants as your design calls for.

A larger consideration is the design aesthetic and growing philosophy you want to adopt. The further your design departs from the natural environment, the more maintenance you will have to do. Look for the right balance between letting mother nature reclaim your site and planting with the purpose of reducing the amount of watering, mowing, and maintenance required. Planting intentionally to foster earth-centered and natural landscapes is more sustainable than following traditional landscape standards. It is one small contribution we can make to protecting our planet.

Know Your Purpose and Markets

If your goal is to sell your lavender, choose plants with attributes that give them crossover markets and uses. Choosing cultivars that perform well in many markets will help you maximize your market opportunities. Some good examples are *Lavandula angustifolia* 'Folgate' (bundles, culinary), *L. angustifolia* 'Royal Velvet' (bundles, buds, oil), and *L. ×intermedia* 'Impress Purple' (bundles, buds, oil).

The market potential of your crops depends on your desires and resources. Selling a minimally handled crop is uncomplicated, but it generally fetches a lower price than a product that has some added value. Whether through packaging or complementary ingredients, you can transform dried lavender or essential oil to add value. For example, if you put crafting buds from lavandin cultivars such as 'Impress Purple' into sachets, you can earn five to six times more than if you sell plain, clean buds by the pound. If you put culinary buds from cultivars like *L. angustifolia* 'Folgate' into a spice bottle or herb blend, you can sell them for six to seven times more per pound than the buds alone.

Because lavender is a versatile crop that can be made into many different products, it offers many different marketing opportunities. You can tackle all the product types and market them to the world, or you can narrow your production down to one product and do quite well. Following are some ideas about potential products and markets to help you clarify your goals.

ESSENTIAL OIL AND HYDROSOL

Grow cultivars that have high essential oil yields and balanced chemical constituents.

PRODUCT IDEAS: perfume, soaps, lotions, balms, linen sprays, hydrosol, and other skin-care products

MARKETS: farm-direct, skin-care manufacturers, healing arts and alternative medicine, aromatherapy industry

CULTIVAR EXAMPLES: *L. angustifolia* 'Maillette' and 'Hidcote Pink'; *L. ×intermedia* 'Grosso' and 'Super'

CRAFTING

Grow lavenders chosen for scent and color of the lavender in its dried form. For bundles, go with cultivars that have less shattering of buds and longer stems.

PRODUCT IDEAS: sachets, soap, pillows, potpourri, dried lavender bundles, wreaths, and flower arrangements

MARKETS: farm-direct, processors, specialty retailers

CULTIVAR EXAMPLES: *L. angustifolia* 'Betty's Blue', 'Royal Velvet', and 'Lavang 21' (Violet Intrigue); *L. ×intermedia* 'Provence', 'Impress Purple', and 'Riverina Thomas'

CULINARY

Choose cultivars for color, scent, and flavor.

PRODUCT IDEAS: baked goods, spice blends, tea blends, chocolates, baking extracts, flavored simple syrups, flavored oils, herb essence beverages

MARKETS: food and beverage processors, manufacturers, and herb distributers that incorporate lavender flavor in their products, such as bakeries, syrup manufacturers, wineries, breweries, and chocolatiers

CULTIVAR EXAMPLES: *L. angustifolia* 'Melissa', 'Folgate', and 'Royal Velvet'

FLORAL

Grow cultivars that have longer and thicker stems, that have desirable flower colors, and that maintain vibrant color when the flowers are dried.

> PRODUCT IDEAS: fresh-cut bouquets, dried bouquets, dried buds
>
> MARKETS: florists, wedding industry, farmers markets, mail-order retailers, brick-and-mortar retailers
>
> CULTIVAR EXAMPLES: *L. angustifolia* 'Betty's Blue', 'Riverina Thomas', 'Royal Velvet', and 'Lavang 21' (Violet Intrigue); *L. ×intermedia* 'Provence' and 'Impress Purple'

AGRITOURISM

Choose cultivars based on creating a succession of blooms to prolong your bloom time. The longer bloom you have, the longer you can offer classes using fresh lavender and U-cut opportunities. Grow lavender cultivars with contrasting colors, long stems, and varying uses.

> PRODUCT IDEAS: Create an experience and a destination to draw people to you. Activities could include painting and yoga in the lavender fields, U-cut lavender, and selling photo passes that permit visitors to take photos during the "golden hours" when you would generally be closed. Create a calendar of events, including wreath making, gardening and cooking classes, and body-care crafting. Give classes and instruction in making soap, bath bombs, shower steamers, and balms, and in incorporating lavender essential oil in your everyday life.
>
> MARKETS: general public, travelers, crafters, gardeners, cooks, lavender enthusiasts
>
> CULTIVAR EXAMPLES: any double-blooming lavender such as *L. angustifolia* 'Buena Vista', 'Lavang 21' (Violet Intrigue), 'Royal Velvet', 'Baby Colby', 'Forever Blue', and 'SuperBlue'; midseason-bloom lavandin cultivars and true lavenders like 'Grosso', 'Impress Purple', and 'Hidcote Giant'

One agritourism idea is permitting visitors or professional photographers to take photos using your lavender as a backdrop.

OTHER LAVENDER FARMS

Many times, lavender farms do not have enough of their own lavender to fulfill their market needs. Often, they can be your best customers. You can grow specifically for other growers and become a supplier of products and services, or you can source an outside supply to complement their own supply and be able to provide lavender year-round to them.

> PRODUCT IDEAS: bundles, buds, and lavender plants; private labeling and crop processing services

Design for Access

When you know your goals and purposes, you can design your planting to take these into consideration. Think about not only the visual aspect of the planting but also how you are going to access and maintain it. For example, the spacing between plant centers will affect how accessible the plants will be for harvesting and how irrigation will be set up, whether furrow or drip irrigation. If you live in an area with considerable rainfall and do not need to irrigate your plants, your choice of what to grow between and around plantings will be broader and could include, for example, growing native or orchard grasses in between rows (intercropping).

INSIDER tip

In the dry climate where I am, I have intercropped with spring wildflowers like poppies. This is also a way of suppressing spring weeds. I knock down the poppies after they have finished blooming and the plant material has dried out and lays flat, adding organic material to the soil. Studies are being done on using buffalo grass for intercropping in arid climates.

When designing access to your lavender patch or large lavender garden, consider how you will enter the patch or garden to prune, harvest your flowers, and maintain the space in between the plantings. If you will use machinery to control weeds and harvest flowers, your design will look different from a space where plants will be maintained by hand. If you plan to use machinery like a riding mower or tractor in between rows of plants, the size of your equipment will dictate the space between your rows. You'll want to allow enough space for your machinery's tires to clear the plantings as you drive between rows.

Another consideration is room to enjoy your plantings. If you plan on having visitors to your farm, they may want to linger and sit between the rows and admire the beauty of the bloom. Incorporating enough space in some rows for seating to take in the views is friendly

Leave enough space between rows for machinery tires to clear the plantings.

LAVENDER FOR ALL SEASONS

and welcoming. For agritourism, allow wider centers where you would like walking access. If your aim is U-pick access, create wider rows for ease of entry.

I personally want to use every square inch of my space and give plants the minimum space they require. I base my planting design on how much space the plant needs and how much space I need to walk comfortably through the furrows to harvest flowers when they are in full bloom.

Planting of two species, *L. angustifolia* and *L. ×intermedia*, with forty to forty-five plants in each row. The entire section contains eight hundred plants.

Run the Numbers

When designing your area, the spacing of plants—both the space between plants in one row and the space between rows—will dictate how many plants you will need for your given layout. Take measurements of your space, get out your graph paper and sketch the area with plant positions indicated, and calculate how many plants you will need. This will help you with plant ordering, calculating costs per plant, and eventually calculating your potential yields.

For large-scale growing of lavender, row planting in a rectangular grid works best. This means dividing the growing area into rows and situating plants evenly along each row. Generally, you leave more space between rows for access and less space between plants in the rows.

As an example, let's look at how a 1-acre plot might be planted. An acre is traditionally defined as an area one furlong (660 feet) long by one chain (66 feet) wide. Thus, an acre covers 43,560 square feet (660 feet × 66 feet). But an acre of land can take any number of other shapes. For instance, a square-shaped acre covers an area of 208.71 by 208.71 feet. To find the linear measurements of other rectangular acres, divide 43,560 by the number of feet you want on one side. (For those on the metric system, a hectare equals about 2.5 acres; 1 acre is 4047 square meters and 0.4047 hectares.)

To figure out how many plants per square acre you can accommodate, simply multiply the number of rows by the number of plants per row. To do this, you need to know the length of your rows (which in the case of a square acre is the length of one side of the plot, 208 feet), the spacing between them, and the spacing between the plants in your rows. Plug those numbers into this formula: (row length ÷ space between rows) × (row length ÷ space between plants).

A common choice for lavender growers is to plant on 5-foot centers, meaning they leave 5 feet (1.5 meters) between plant centers for walking paths. In this case, if a bed is 2 feet (24 inches) wide, the walking path is 3 feet wide; if a bed is 2½ feet (30 inches) wide, the walking path is 2½ feet wide. With this spacing, a square acre can

INSIDER tip

Spacing is measured from the center of one plant to the center of an adjoining plant. "Planting on 5-foot centers" means allowing 5 feet between plants in adjoining rows, measured center to center.

accommodate 41 rows (208 feet, the length of one side of the plot and also of the rows, divided by 5 feet). The number of plants that can be grown on a square acre will vary according to the spacing of plants within these rows.

- At 2.5 feet between plants, you would be able to fit 83 plants per row (208 feet, the length of a row, divided by 2.5 feet), for a total of 3403 plants (83 plants × 41 rows).
- At 3 feet between plants, you could grow 69 plants per row (208 feet divided by 3 feet), for a total of 2829 plants (69 plants × 41 rows).
- At 4 feet between plants, 52 plants per row (208 divided by 4), for a total of 2132 plants (52 plants × 41 rows).

A six-foot center with varying plant spacing will accommodate a different number of plants and produce different yields per acre. Wider spacing between rows can allow larger equipment to enter between rows.

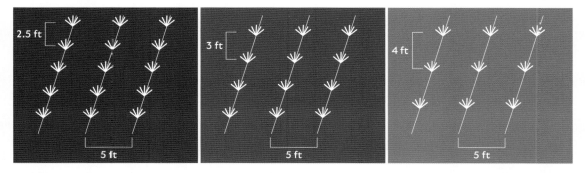

A high-density planting with five-foot centers is an example of a market garden setting or lawn replacement yard. A 90 x 90 feet space would accommodate: 36 plants per row with 2.5 feet space for a total of 640 plants, 30 plants per row with 3 feet spacing for a total of 540 plants, and 24 plants per row with 4 feet spacing for a total of 414 plants.

GROWING LAVENDER ON A LARGER SCALE   169

Equipment Needs

Your farm or garden will differ from others, so whatever equipment you decide to invest in will be unique to your given situation. Your choice of tools and equipment is as broad as your own imagination, whether you are a lavender enthusiast with a lavender patch or owner of a multi-acre operation.

My farm, where we grow more than nineteen thousand lavender plants, is a patchwork of different areas, from multiple planted acres to small demonstration gardens, and my equipment varies for each site.

- To distill essential oil and hydrosol, I use a 35- or 100-gallon (130- or 380-L) still.
- To remove the buds from the stems, I use a motorized chimney brush.
- To process lavender buds, I use a seed cleaner that can clean 30 to 50 pounds of buds at one time.
- To shape my beds, I use my low-horsepower tractor fitted with a bed-forming attachment.
- To till small-space plantings or single rows and form beds, I use a rototiller.
- For harvesting, I use a hand sickle.
- For weed control, I use woven fabric and natural mulch.
- To prune, I use a motorized hedge trimmer.
- To automate the harvest and prune on a larger scale, I use a harvester attachment that can double as a pruner.

Anatomy of a Lavender Planting

A successful lavender planting starts with a plan that maps out cultivated areas and mulched or uncultivated areas, defines a soil improvement strategy, and selects plants based on growing zone and plant function. It also includes water-saving strategies, an irrigation plan, and a long-term maintenance plan. As an example, let's walk through a field on my farm as I prepare it for lavender beds.

DESIGN AND SPACING

This field is a small patch that can be highly productive and aesthetically pleasing at the same time. The site has a slightly downward slope that facilitates good drainage, along with beautiful views of Grand Mesa to the east and Mount Garfield to the north. I want the area to serve multiple purposes, both in its use and the type of lavender I harvest. I want a uniform look with some small design elements, a midseason bloom for my farm visitors to have the opportunity to cut their own bundles, and an area where friends and visitors can hang out and enjoy sitting or strolling amidst lavender while taking in magnificent views.

I choose to plant on 5-foot centers and space the plants 3 feet apart in their rows in order to maximize the planting and create a uniform look. At the center of the rectangle, I will leave a 7-foot-wide row to accommodate a foot path and comfortable seating. The 7-foot-wide center row will draw people in and limit where they can wander. There will be a center circle with hay bales arranged for seating that provides a place for people to take photographs of the blooming lavender with the mountainous backdrop.

The space measures 80 feet by 175 feet. Based on 5-foot centers, the plot can accommodate 16 rows (80 divided by 5), and each row, with plants spaced 3 feet apart, can hold 58 plants (175 divided by 3), for a total of 928 plants (16 times 58).

SOIL AND FIELD PREPARATION

To prepare the new area for lavender planting, we begin in winter by first removing old, unproductive cherry trees. We leave orchard grasses and clover, which we plan to till in spring. The area has been a no-till cherry orchard for more than twenty years, so the soil has been compacted by years of tractor and foot traffic. The tree trunks must be pulled and the heavy clay soil loosened. We "rip" the soil in the early spring, which means we till it deeply using strong tines that penetrate the compact soil and mechanically break up and shatter any hardpan.

We follow up with disking and using a spring-tooth harrow to smooth the soil. This mechanical work helps improve drainage for the upcoming lavender planting. The soil has plenty of organic matter, and according to a soil analysis the area has the appropriate nutrients for lavender, so other than making the soil workable, nothing else needs to be done.

Prepared field ready to be worked for beds.

Once fields are tilled and large rocks removed, it's time to form the beds. My clay loam soil dictates using mounded beds to make sure all the plants have good drainage. We use a bed-former attachment on the tractor, a very quick and easy way to create a raised bed when working with a larger space. Some bed shapers are built to lay mulch and emitter tubing at the same time as forming the bed.

clockwise from top:

Forming beds with a tractor attachment called a bed former or bed shaper.

We set the bed former to make the beds 30 inches wide.

With heavier soils, our beds need to be at least 8 inches deep.

PLANT SELECTION

My USDA zone is favorable for both *Lavandula angustifolia* and *Lavandula ×intermedia*. I choose the *L. ×intermedia* cultivars 'Riverina Thomas' and 'Edelweiss'. 'Riverina Thomas' has long, beautiful stems with large spikes, making it ideal for fresh-cut and dried bundles, crafting buds, and essential oil. 'Edelweiss' is a white-flowering lavandin that I will use to line the 7-foot-wide path, making a border that will contrast beautifully with the purple-violet blooms of 'Riverina Thomas'. These two lavandins can also be used to make lovely essential oils and hydrosol if not all the flowers are harvested for fresh-cut or dried bundles.

I will plant the last row to the west along the orchard with *L. angustifolia* 'Irene Doyle', a continuous double bloomer. This row will border the outside of the rectangle, which serves as a pathway to another field beyond the orchard and the new planting. The blooms of this cultivar will be used for essential oil and hydrosol.

A fresh-cut bundle of *Lavandula ×intermedia* 'Riverina Thomas', a triploid hybrid that can produce two to three times more essential oil than typical lavandins and has a large spike.

The outside border areas will be seeded with a dwarf, low-growing white clover (*Trifolium repens*), which requires a minimal amount of water and mowing and makes a lush border that people can walk or sit on to lounge and picnic.

IRRIGATION AND LONG-TERM MAINTENANCE

To control weeds and minimize maintenance, I use weed fabric in the furrows. I leave the space open between plants to optimize ventilation and ensure soil and plant health. To conserve water and minimize weeds, I plan to use drip irrigation. Taking into consideration long-term maintenance of the planting, I place the emitter tubing on top of the soil so I can quickly troubleshoot any malfunctioning emitters. I anchor the irrigation lines to ensure they won't move with any shrinking and expanding created by the varying temperatures throughout the year. We can have a 35-degree temperature differential in one day!

Even though I use filters in the drip system, I have to be careful of built-up sediment. Because our water comes from the Colorado River, fine particles accumulate in the lines throughout the season. I place flush valves at the end of each line to rinse out any accumulated sediments. I place a valve at the beginning of each line in case I need to restrict watering to any given row. I have found that these

The field planted according to plan.

maintenance nuances make a difference and move me closer to a long-lasting and successful planting.

After one full calendar year of growth, this field is well on its way to high-yield production. It gave us more than 1.5 gallons (5680 ml) of essential oil, 16 gallons (60,550 ml) of hydrosol, fifty U-cut bundles, and 5 pounds (2.27 kg) of crafting buds. It also provides a beautiful landscape for our visitors and friends to enjoy. They will be able to meander and pick fresh lavender for many years to come.

above left: Weed fabric laid and secured with landscape staples in furrows and the center walkway.

above right: Drip irrigation laid on top of the beds with an emitter going to each plant, six weeks after the plants went into the ground from 4-inch pots.

left: The field in late spring, six weeks after planting.

below left: The field a year and four months later, after the first harvest.

below right: A view of the field from the other side.

Planning for Increasing Yields

When my first large planting of lavender was four years old, I was overwhelmed by the number of fresh-cut bundles I needed to hang and dry. The drying racks in my small barn were loaded with bundles that could not dry fast enough to accommodate more bundles coming in from the field. I had bundles hanging in every nook and cranny of the farm and small portable wire racks under every roof. I finally had to rent a neighbor's shed and convert it to a drying shed so I could control the ventilation and temperature. My hand debudding system and small cleaning screens had to be converted quickly to a mechanized cleaning and screening system.

As your plants get larger, expect your lavender harvest to grow. Harvest yields depend on species, cultivar, growing zones, and conditions. Fully understanding the potential yields from each species will help you plan for larger harvests to come. The good news is there is a bit of time to work out the details for handling more lavender. A plant takes five years to become fully grown, so make sure to prepare for more processing space, time, and labor as your plants flourish.

Here are some examples of what to expect (note that a bundle contains approximately seventy-five stems):

LAVANDULA ×INTERMEDIA CULTIVARS

year 1	0–1 bundle per plant
year 2	2–3 bundles per plant
year 3	4–6 bundles per plant
year 4	7–10 bundles per plant
year 5	9–12 bundles per plant

LAVANDULA ANGUSTIFOLIA, MEDIUM-SIZE TO LARGE CULTIVARS

year 1	0–1 bundle per plant
year 2	1–2 bundles per plant
year 3	2–4 bundles per plant
year 4	3–5 bundles per plant
year 5	5–8 bundles per plant

Propagating Lavender

Learning how to propagate is important for any gardener and lavender grower, as it is a way you can expand your lavender plantings without spending money on nursery plants. Plus, lavender plants make wonderful gifts; any extra plants you grow can be shared with friends. Add a nice touch by giving them growing instructions along with the plant.

You can propagate lavender in fall and winter in any hardiness zone, and in spring in USDA zones 7 and above. Every fall and winter, we propagate thousands of lavender plants from cuttings. The process is simple, with just a few key things to remember.

Propagation from cuttings maintains the true characteristics of any particular cultivar. Lavender grown from seed will not hold the true traits of the mother plant and is considered to be variable. This is because cross-pollination by bees occurs, thus "hybridizing" the seed produced from the plant; those seeds then grow into plants with traits different from the original plant. Growing lavender from nonhybridized seed can be challenging. If you attempt it, a brisk scarification with fine sandpaper can help, followed by sowing in sandy soil and keeping the medium moist and cool until seeds germinate, which can take four to six weeks.

If you grow *Lavandula stoechas*, you may find tiny plants starting at the base of the plant. Stoechas are also known to self-seed and can be grown from seed or from softwood cuttings.

Some lavender species are easy to root and others are not. *Lavandula* ×*intermedia* cultivars root faster than *L. angustifolia* cultivars, and *L. angustifolia* 'Buena Vista' is particularly difficult to propagate. Cuttings generally take anywhere from two to six weeks to root, although some cultivars can take eight to twelve weeks. *Lavandula* ×*intermedia* cultivars like 'Grosso', 'Super', and 'Impress Purple' are easy to propagate and take ten to twelve days to root.

Propagation success rates will vary, depending on the species, cultivar, and age of the plant you take cuttings from. To help

Sometimes you may notice variations called sports cropping up in your garden or field. These are the result of random, naturally occurring genetic mutation and not due to cross-pollination. Such cellular mutations can change the appearance of the foliage, flowers, fruit, or stems of any plant. Many times, the variation will disappear after a while.

A spotted sport I found in my field. Very entertaining!

Rooted 1-inch lavender plugs await transplanting into individual pots.

guarantee you will end up with the number of plants you hope to produce, when cutting in fall take 25 percent more cuttings of *L. ×intermedia* and 50 to 100 percent more cuttings of *L. angustifolia* than you think you will need.

PLANT PATENTS AND PROPAGATION

Some plant varieties are protected as intellectual property through various types of patents. Plant patents apply primarily to perennial fruits and ornamentals that are propagated from cuttings or by tubers. Their use or propagation may be restricted by the patent owner. Such restrictions determine whether you can propagate the variety for your own use or to sell commercially. Varieties not under such protection are held in the public domain and can be used and propagated without restrictions.

Patents and their restrictions can vary from country to country. In the United States, plant patents are regulated by the US Patent and Trademark Office (USPTO). The patent holder has the "right to exclude" (without permission) others from reproducing the protected material for a period of twenty years. To verify if a lavender cultivar has a patent or trademark, enter the cultivar name in the Google Patents search box at patents.google.com.

KEYS TO SUCCESSFUL PROPAGATION

Successful propagation requires five key elements: quality cutting material, a sterile growing medium, and adequate light, heat, and moisture.

QUALITY CUTTING MATERIAL. Use healthy, disease-free cuttings from nonflowering plants. Vigorous shoots from younger plants make ideal cuttings. Older plants have more woody growth and may not root as readily, although woody growth can be used in early winter propagation. Pruning plants lightly in fall can promote enough growth on the side shoots to take cuttings in fall and early winter. To have lavender ready for spring planting, take cuttings in fall and winter. For fall planting, take cuttings in spring.

STERILE GROWING MEDIUM. The ideal medium for growing plants does not involve soil and thus can be free of weeds, insects, and diseases. A light, highly porous, sterile soilless medium is a must! This is especially important for lavender stems since they like good drainage. Rooting can be slowed if the substrate is too heavy and retains too much water. A desirable substrate is generally more porous than media used in finished containers or pots. An ideal growing medium for your

Propagation Terminology

Some terms come up again and again in propagation, and I think it's empowering for lavender growers of all scales to familiarize themselves with the lexicon.

CUTTINGS are pieces of a plant's stem taken for the purpose of propagating the plant by rooting them in a growth medium such as moist soil.

HARDWOOD (RIPE) CUTTINGS are cuttings taken from inside a plant, three or four nodes up from the wood, while the plant is dormant and shows no sign of active growth, in late fall, winter, or early spring.

SEMI-HARDWOOD CUTTINGS are taken in midsummer or early fall from the current season's growth, when the wood is reasonably firm and the leaves are of mature size.

SOFTWOOD CUTTINGS are cuttings of soft new growth taken in spring or fall. The soft shoots are quite tender, and extra care must be taken to keep them from drying out, but they tend to root more quickly than other cuttings.

CALLUS FORMATION refers to the formation of tissue to protect the wound where a stem was cut. Plants form a callus before putting out a root, and roots are produced from the callus tissue.

LEAF NODE refers to the small swelling that is part of a plant stem from which leaves emerge. It is a site of cellular activity and growth, where small buds develop into leaves, stems, or flowers. When making a cutting for propagation, it is important to locate a plant's nodes, making a cut just above, but not too close to, a node.

NEW GROWTH refers to the tips of stems produced in the current growing season.

ROOTING HORMONE is a naturally occurring or synthetic hormone that stimulates root growth in plants. The main rooting hormone for vegetative plant material is **AUXIN**; it causes the elongation of cells in shoots and helps regulate plant growth.

From left to right: a hardwood cutting, a semi-hardwood cutting, and a softwood cutting.

Callus formation: right stem, no callus; middle stem, callus forming; left stem, root beginning to develop.

GROWING LAVENDER ON A LARGER SCALE

cuttings consists of 40 to 50 percent sphagnum peat moss to retain moisture, 30 to 50 percent small-to-medium-size horticultural perlite (expanded lava rock) or small lava rock to ensure good drainage, and a small amount of dolomitic limestone to neutralize acids in the growing medium and provide some additional magnesium and calcium for plant uptake. Note that vermiculite is not recommended as it retains more moisture than lavender likes. Peat moss poses environmental challenges as it is slow to renew, so sometimes coconut coir is used as a replacement, but coir retains more moisture than peat moss. If you prefer to use a coir-based growing medium, use a smaller percentage of coir in your mix and a larger percentage of perlite or lava rock. If you use peat moss, do not use it in large quantities and purchase from a reputable source.

LIGHT. Light promotes photosynthesis and even plant growth, which produces strong stems and roots. Plants need less light for cell division to occur when they are forming a callus. Once the cutting has formed roots, you can increase the light. If you do not have a place to set the cuttings with evenly distributed light and enough light intensity and duration, you may need to add grow lights.

HEAT. Rooting of cuttings is encouraged by moisture, warmth, and good aeration. Callus formation is primarily driven by temperature. You want to maintain your growing medium at 75 to 80 degrees F (24 to 27 degrees C). For the gardener, this usually requires using a heat mat under trays; for the grower, floor or under-bench heating. The air temperature should be 5 to 10 degrees F (2.7 to 5.5 degrees C) below that of the soil to ensure that root growth is more rapid than shoot growth. For example, if your heat mat is set at a constant 75 degrees F (24 degrees C), keep your ambient temperature at 65 degrees F (18.5 degrees C).

MOISTURE AND HUMIDITY. Keep your starts moist but do not overwater; stems can rot. Most plants enjoy a humidity of 50 to 60 percent. You can create humidity by covering your propagation tray with a plastic dome. In a greenhouse setting, mist your greenhouse to add humidity when it begins to warm up, and vent the hot air outside. Installing a misting system is one option, or you can use a misting attachment on your hose. Spraying the floor with water in the morning will also raise the humidity levels during the day, and circulating fans can control and alleviate humidity when it's too humid. Only mist during the day, because too much humidity as the greenhouse cools at night can encourage disease.

PROPAGATING LAVENDER, STEP BY STEP

Have these materials on hand:

- clean pruning snips or garden scissors with precision blades
- disinfectant such as 70 percent isopropyl alcohol
- draining growing tray no more than 2 inches deep, and/or a plug tray insert with 72, 98, or 128 1-inch cells
- sterile, porous soilless potting mix
- rooting hormone (optional)
- seedling heat mat with temperature controller

above: Materials for propagation: precision pruning snips or garden scissors and disinfectant.

left: A 4-inch lavender plant that was propagated in a 72-cell tray.

GROWING LAVENDER ON A LARGER SCALE

1. Fill the seed starter tray with soilless potting mix and then water so the medium is moist all the way through.

2. Sterilize your pruning snips or garden scissors in preparation for taking cuttings in the field as well as cutting the material you stick in your propagation tray.

3. In the garden or field, cut healthy, straight, and vigorous stems just below a leaf node for rooting. Plants or stems that are free of blooms are best for hardwood cuttings. If you must use a flowering stem, cut off the top before placing it in your tray. Healthy new growth is best for semi-hardwood and softwood cuttings.

above left: Sterilize cutting implements by spraying with 70 percent isopropyl alcohol.

above right: The ideal hardwood cutting is free of blooms.

right: Look for healthy new growth for softwood cuttings.

182   LAVENDER FOR ALL SEASONS

④ Remove all leaves from the lower 2 to 3 inches of stem, depending on the size of the cutting. Leaf removal will naturally score the stem (make slight slits vertically) unless you are working with very woody material. In the latter case, you can use a razor blade to remove the outer layer of the stem ¼ to ½ inch from the bottom of the cutting. Scoring the stem exposes more surface area for rooting.

⑤ Cut the end of the stem at a 45-degree angle. This slight slant maximizes the area exposed for rooting.

⑥ If you are working with a *Lavandula ×intermedia* cutting, trim the tips of the leaves. This step is unnecessary for softwood cuttings.

above left: Remove lower leaves from the stem.

above right: Cut the end of the stem at a 45-degree angle.

left: Trim the tips of the leaves of a *Lavandula ×intermedia* cutting.

GROWING LAVENDER ON A LARGER SCALE

INSIDER tip

If your lavender starts do not root, the problem may be the size of the container, the density of the growing medium, or the amount of light they're getting. It's best to use a seed starter tray with 1-inch cells or an open tray no more than 2 inches deep for stem cuttings so that when the tray is placed on a heating mat, the heat can penetrate the soil medium and reach the root zone. Use a sterile and highly porous potting mix to avoid causing root rot and disease. Spindly and uneven plant growth may be caused by uneven light and/or not enough light, so I recommend using a greenhouse or grow lights.

7. Optional: dip the end of the cutting in hormone gel or rooting powder or an organic natural rooting hormone. This is not a necessary step with lavender unless you are using a very woody cutting or dormant cuttings.

8. Insert the end of the cutting into your moistened growing medium.

9. Place the full tray on a heated mat. The key to helping the cutting take root is to maintain the heat at 75 to 80 degrees F (24 to 27 degrees C) until cell division occurs and roots begin to form. This can take a few weeks; you can check for roots by tugging very gently on the cutting or lifting the tray to see if roots are growing outside it.

10. Once you have a healthy rooted cutting, pot it up into a sterilized 2½-inch-to-4-inch pot filled with a porous, well-draining potting mix. You can add a slow-release fertilizer to the potting mix or apply a liquid fertilizer every four weeks. You can also add beneficial organisms such as beneficial bacteria, trichoderma, or mycorrhizae; mycorrhizal fungi become an extension of the plant's root system that will broaden the plant's access to vital nutrients and water when it is transplanted. These organisms can be purchased in granular form and added to the soil mix at the application rate recommended on the package, either when potting up or when transplanting starts in the ground.

11. Maintain an ambient temperature of 65 to 72 degrees F (18.5 to 22 degrees C) and provide full consistent light until plants have established a healthy root system. Trim any flower buds with stems that may be forming, in order to encourage side branching.

12. Harden off or acclimate your potted plants by setting them outside for one week, day and night, after the last frost, and then transplant them into the ground. If the weather should unexpectedly dip below freezing while the plants are hardening off, cover them or shelter them inside.

Insert your cutting into the moistened growing medium.

Maintain the temperature of your growing medium at 75 to 80 degrees F (24 to 27 degrees C).

Chapter 6

Cooking with Lavender

When I first started my lavender farm, I educated myself on using lavender and its different species in cooking, as well as inviting the visitors who came to the farm to sample sweet and savory dishes. I came across many people who had had a negative experience tasting lavender and hesitated to try anything with lavender in it. Once I questioned them, it came out that they had eaten or drunk something that had either had too much lavender, used the wrong species of lavender, or contained an overabundance of whole lavender buds. No one wants that! But there are so many beautiful ways to enjoy lavender in food.

My approach in this chapter is not to give you a million recipes but to show you how to incorporate lavender in the dishes you already cook. More important, it is to demystify lavender and urge you to consider it as a culinary herb. Adding lavender to sweet or savory dishes or beverages will elevate your cuisine to a new level.

Lida Lafferty, author of *Spike It with Lavender: Recipes for Living*, told me:

Lavender is the conductor in the medley of ingredients. It's a guiding light of flavor. Tread gently. A little goes a long way. The colors are mesmerizing in the field or in the garden, in the dried buds in the jar or in the jam. The aroma is tantalizing as the oven door opens on a roasted lavender loaf of sourdough bread. Or how about when you brush past a blooming plant on a pathway or after a soft rain or simply pinching a bud. Bring those moments to your dish!

Lavender as a Culinary Herb

Lavender is a flowering herb. The calyx is what we cook with and where most of the flavors originate. The corolla comes out of the calyx with a distinct corolla tube and five fused petals that generally fall out of the calyx when the lavender dries. These petals do not have essence but in fresh form make a nice edible flower decoration. Besides, you can use lavender stems and leaves the same way you would when cooking with rosemary, as a seasoning that has a woodsy fragrance and piney flavor.

While lavender is more delicate in flavor than its minty counterparts, it is best used in moderation. It is easier to add as you go than try to adjust the recipe once you have added too much. Recipes are made to be adapted, more lavender or less according to your taste buds. Be brave! Experiment!

With that in mind, you can explore endless possibilities. Not only can you use lavender in cookies and cakes, it also pairs well with rich and fatty foods, cutting through and lifting the overall flavor. For example, lavender can be infused into cream that can be added to pudding, custard, crème fraîche, ice cream, or whipped cream. Blended with other herbs, lavender can be stuffed underneath the skin of roasted chicken. Later in this chapter you'll find many more suggestions for adding lavender to foods.

WHICH SPECIES TO COOK WITH?

What makes "culinary" lavender culinary? This is among the top questions I receive from customers and lavender enthusiasts, second only to the question of how to grow lavender. People ask me, "What is culinary lavender?" and "What is the difference between that and other lavender?" My answer is: all lavender is edible but not all is palatable.

Lavender is an herb with flowers that can impart a delicate flavor to foods.

Each species has its own levels of chemical compounds, as discussed in chapter 1. Some are more pleasing than others in both aroma and taste. *Lavandula ×intermedia* (lavandin), *L. lanata*, *L. dentata*, and *L. stoechas* all have high levels of 1,8-cineole (eucalyptol) and camphor, giving them a strong, astringent aroma and bitter taste, so in general these are not species with culinary uses. However, some *L. ×intermedia* cultivars such as 'Gros Bleu' and 'Provence' have lower levels of camphor and eucalyptol than others in the species, making them more pleasant to cook with, especially when paired with rosemary, sage, and thyme, and added to meats such as beef and chicken.

The most delightful species to cook with is *Lavandula angustifolia*, or true lavender, due to its higher levels of linalyl acetate and linalool and its lower levels of terpinen-4-ol. Within that species, varying levels of linalyl acetate make a cultivar more or less floral, with 'Royal Velvet' and 'Sharon Roberts' being examples of those with more floral notes in flavor and scent. Cultivars that are balanced in their dominant compounds, like 'Melissa' and 'Croxton's Wild', have a bit of a spice note. The table in chapter 2 showing the best uses of *L. angustifolia* cultivars indicates which ones have culinary uses.

FRESH OR DRIED?

Fresh lavender isn't only a beautiful garnish; you can use fresh lavender as you would other fresh herbs like rosemary, thyme, or sage. Fresh lavender infuses more quickly and is more pungent than the dried form, although the fresh form is less concentrated. Dried lavender buds are three times more concentrated than fresh blooming lavender in a dish. Generally, you would use two to three times more fresh than dried lavender buds in a recipe.

Since its bloom is seasonal, fresh lavender is not always readily available like dried is, but it is equally as wonderful to cook with. Fresh lavender works especially well if you are roasting meats like lamb, chicken, pork, or beef, or vegetables such as sweet potatoes and carrots. Trim the stems and use only the portion with buds.

CAN YOU COOK WITH ESSENTIAL OIL?

I am often asked if you can cook or flavor foods with lavender essential oil. The answer has two parts: yes, you can, but the flavor is a bit different from that imparted by using the plant material. The flavor profile differs because the plant's

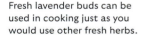

Fresh lavender buds can be used in cooking just as you would use other fresh herbs.

essential oils are highly concentrated. I have found it much easier to achieve a lavender flavor using lavender in the herb form than in the essential oil form. If you want to experiment with using essential oil in cooking, always use it sparingly: one drop at a time and always diluted with other ingredients. If the recipe calls for cream, olive oil, or butter, dilute your essential oil by adding it to these fats first.

FOOD PARTNERS

Go beyond traditional food pairings by thinking about the molecular level of what makes great combinations. The dominant chemical compounds found in lavender's aroma are also found in lavender's flavor: linalyl acetate, linalool, and terpinen-4-ol. These same compounds are found in other herbs, spices, and foods. Often foods with the same compounds can pair well.

Lavender's primary aromas are floral, fruity, herbaceous, spicy, and medicinal. Complementary ingredients that match well with the flavors and aromas of lavender include honey, elderberry, lemon, cream, and sugar. Herbs that pair well are caraway, rosemary, savory, and thyme. Spices that are great partners include salt, star anise, nutmeg, allspice, vanilla, and cacao.

Lavender complements certain fruits very well. These include citrus, most dried fruits, melon, and flowering tree fruits such as almonds, peaches, nectarines, plums, cherries, apricots, pears, apples, and figs. For example, you can balance lavender's medium notes with something bright like lemon or orange juice and zest. All root vegetables, especially potatoes and sweet potatoes, are friends with lavender. All varieties of meat pair beautifully with lavender, especially lamb, chicken, and oily fishes like salmon.

The Lavender Grower's Pantry

To add an overall flavor of lavender to a dish, you will use infusions, extracts, and ground lavender. You can infuse, extract, and grind lavender ahead of time to have on hand when you want to incorporate it as a wet or dry ingredient in recipes. When you have all your basic ingredients prepared, it is easy to make any recipe.

Infusion is steeping buds in a liquid such as boiling water, warmed cream or milk, honey, maple syrup, vinegar, or oil before adding the liquid to your food. Measure 1 tablespoon of dried buds or 2 tablespoons of fresh buds per 1 cup of liquid.

Steep for ten to fifteen minutes in hot liquids or up to one week in cool liquids; if left longer, it can create a bitter flavor. Honey or maple syrup are more forgiving on this score.

Infusing dry-roasted lavender buds is a quick way to flavor olive oils. Dry roast the buds by adding them to a dry skillet on low to medium heat for one to two minutes. Then heat the olive oil and pour it over the dry-roasted buds. Keep the mixture on medium-high heat for two minutes and then turn off the heat and strain out the buds, and you are left with a wonderfully flavored oil that you can incorporate in any recipe.

Extraction is steeping buds in high-proof alcohol like vodka or an alcohol alternative over a long period of time. Lavender extract can be made with fresh or dried lavender buds. Gently press the buds using a mortar and pestle to release their flavor and fragrance before steeping. Lavender extract is less concentrated than essential oil but more concentrated than the fresh herb. Add lavender extract as you would add any other extract to any baking recipe.

Grinding is pulverizing dried buds in an herb grinder, food processor, or clean coffee grinder. You can also gently press the lavender with a mortar and pestle to grind it. Grinding is an easy way to ensure even distribution of the buds when added to herb and spice blends like chili and lemon pepper, or to lavender sugar. You can also add ground buds to the dry ingredients of a baking recipe.

Grind several tablespoons of lavender buds in a clean coffee or spice grinder and store in an airtight container so that you will have the ground buds on hand whenever you need them. If your grinder does not pulverize the buds, try using one teaspoon of granulated sugar to one tablespoon of lavender for those sweet recipes that call for sugar. Grinding the buds with a little bit of sugar helps the buds grind fine and eliminates any coarse pieces.

Insider tip

Generally, you do not want to use whole lavender buds in a recipe. The exceptions are when you are adding very few buds to an herb blend, like herbes de Provence, or using a very light sprinkling of buds on a dessert such as a pie. In these cases, you want to limit the distribution of buds to one to two buds per bite, no more.

Useful Tools for Adding Lavender to Foods

I find that having certain tools—most of which are probably already handy in your kitchen—aids in incorporating lavender into recipes. The following are some of my favorites.

- **TEA INFUSER OR CHEESECLOTH.** A wire mesh or perforated ball that holds tea leaves is a great tool to hold lavender buds for infusion in cream, milk, or hot water. If you do not have a tea infuser, you can use cheesecloth to steep dried lavender buds in liquid.

- **FINE-MESH SIEVE.** A sieve with smaller openings removes the fine particles left behind from lavender buds. This is especially useful when you are making a simple syrup. Strain the finished syrup through the mesh to remove the buds and you will be left with a beautiful pink-purple liquid. Use a more open mesh when straining hot oils from lavender.

- **COFFEE FILTER.** A simple plastic coffee filter or stainless-steel funnel lined with an unbleached paper coffee filter can be used to strain out lavender buds or particles when making extracts or hydrosols.

- **SPICE GRINDER OR COFFEE GRINDER.** I like to have a dedicated lavender grinder that is not contaminated with the residue of coffee beans. (To remove residue from a grinder, grind one tablespoon of dry rice and then wipe out.)

- **PEPPER AND SALT MILLS.** Adding lavender buds to peppercorns or salt in a mill is a great way to incorporate a dash of freshly ground dried lavender in a dish.

- **MORTAR AND PESTLE.** A mortar is a heavy bowl, usually made of stone, used to grind spices and herbs. The pestle is the club-shaped implement used to do the grinding. Both should be made of a nonporous material like marble or stone; this is easy to clean and does not hold any residues of flavors and aromas. A mortar and pestle is also useful when you want to gently press lavender buds to release their aromatic oils.

- **GLASS CONTAINERS OR JARS.** Glass containers or jars are the best way to store flavored sugars, herb blends, and other pantry creations. Clear or amber glass are my favorites.

From left to right: lavender cocoa, lavender sugar, infused lavender sugar, lavender syrup.

SUGARS AND SYRUPS

Sugar can be flavored with lavender and other complementary flavors. Once you get familiar with lavender pairings, the possibilities and flavors are limitless. You can use lavender sugar as a substitute in any recipe that calls for sugar, especially recipes that contain chocolate, lemon, or orange. Try it in sugar cookies and add to quick breads, muffins, scones, and tea. You can also infuse lavender into syrup or honey to mix with lemonade, iced tea, coffee, cocktails, or even meringue. When presented in a decorative jar or bottle, lavender sugars and syrups make an attractive gift for the holidays.

Ground Lavender Sugar

Grinding lavender buds with sugar before adding the lavender sugar to a recipe allows for an even distribution of flavor.

1 teaspoon dried culinary lavender buds

1 cup granulated sugar

Combine the dried buds and the sugar in a grinder or food processor. Pulse until finely ground. Store in an airtight container and use for baking and sweetening beverages.

Infused Lavender Sugar

Infusing whole dried lavender buds into sugar allows the natural oils to permeate the sugar crystals. The flavors get stronger over time as the mixture is allowed to sit. The mixture can then be finely ground, or the buds can be sifted out.

3 tablespoons dried culinary lavender buds

2 cups granulated sugar

Stir the dried buds into the granulated sugar and store in an airtight container. Leave the mixture to blend for a week or two. Finely grind the mixture in a grinder or food processor, or use a fine-mesh sieve to sift out the buds before using in baked goods and beverages.

Lavender Vanilla Sugar

You can make lavender sugar more complex by adding complementary flavors. Don't stop with vanilla—try adding dried lemon or orange zest to your jar as well.

1 vanilla bean, minced

3 tablespoons dried culinary lavender buds

2 cups granulated sugar, divided

Grind the vanilla bean with the lavender buds and ¼ cup of the sugar in a spice grinder. Whisk this mixture into the remaining 1¾ cups of sugar to thoroughly incorporate. Store in an airtight glass jar.

Lavender Honey

A delightful alternative to lavender sugar and just as versatile. Spread lavender-flavored honey on toast, biscuits, or pancakes. Add to desserts and hot beverages.

3 tablespoons dried culinary lavender buds

1 cup honey

In a wide mouth jar, stir the lavender buds into the honey. Let steep and infuse for one to two weeks, then strain buds from honey using a more open mesh strainer. You can warm the honey first to strain the buds more easily.

Insider tip

For a simple gift kit, stir 6 tablespoons of dried culinary lavender buds into 2 cups of granulated sugar and pour into a decorative jar or bottle. Include instructions on how to prepare lavender syrup, along with a few recipes tied to the bottle.

Simple Lavender Syrup

This simple lavender syrup can be added to coffee, iced or hot tea, lemonade, or your favorite cocktail. The quick method of preparing it uses more lavender buds and takes less time to steep; the slow method uses fewer lavender buds and steeps up to one week before straining. If you'd like a stronger honey flavor, add more honey. Use a 2-to-1 ratio and experiment with different types of honey. For example, orange blossom marries well with lavender.

2 cups water

2 cups sugar or honey

Quick method: ½ cup dried culinary lavender buds

Slow method: ¼ cup dried culinary lavender buds

Bring the water to a boil. Turn off the heat and add the sugar or honey. Stir to dissolve. Add the lavender buds and stir until the buds are completely submerged in the liquid. For the quick method, let the buds steep for one hour. For the slow method, refrigerate and steep for three to seven days. Do not steep longer than that, as the flavor will turn bitter.

Strain out the buds and pour the syrup into a sterilized glass jar. Refrigerate for up to one month or place in a plastic container and freeze for up to six months. Due to the high sugar content, the frozen syrup is easy to scoop. You can also pour the syrup into ice cube trays and freeze, then pop out the cubes and add a cube at a time to any recipe.

CHOCOLATE CREATIONS

The flavors of lavender and chocolate pair beautifully. Think of adding lavender to hot cocoa and chocolate cakes and cookies.

Lavender Cocoa

Having this ready at all times in your cabinet makes life better! For one 8-ounce cup of hot cocoa, add ⅓ cup of the lavender cocoa to ⅔ cup dairy or nondairy milk.

1 tablespoon dried culinary lavender buds, ground

⅔ cup Dutch-process cocoa powder

1 cup confectioners' sugar

Combine the ground buds, cocoa powder, and sugar in a large mixing bowl, and sift through a fine-mesh sieve. Store in an airtight glass container. Add to hot milk or coffee, or dust on cakes and cupcakes.

Lavender Hot Cocoa Mix

I like to use 'Folgate' in this mix as it adds a hint of mint. To use the mix, just add water for a mug of comfort on a cold winter night. It makes enough mix for eight to ten mugs of hot cocoa.

3 tablespoons dried culinary lavender buds

1 cup Dutch-process cocoa powder (for smoother flavor) or natural cocoa powder

2 cups confectioners' sugar

2 cups powdered milk

miniature marshmallows

cacao nibs

Pulse the lavender buds with the cocoa powder in a food processor until ground. Add the confectioners' sugar. Sift the blended ingredients into a large mixing bowl using a fine-mesh sieve, and discard any lavender bud remnants. Add the powdered milk and blend with a hand whisk. Pour into a wide mouth glass jar for storage.

For a rich, thick cup of hot cocoa, place ½ cup of the cocoa mix in your favorite festive mug and add ½ cup boiling water. For a thinner hot cocoa, add 1 cup of boiling water. Sprinkle marshmallows and cacao nibs on top. For a holiday gift, pour the mix into a glass jar and top with marshmallows and cacao nibs, then tie a ribbon around the lid.

COOKING WITH LAVENDER

Pair Lavender and Chocolate in Cookies

This is my all-time and customer favorite recipe. You will impress friends and family when you offer this cookie on its own or used to garnish ice cream. 'Folgate' or 'Melissa' are exceptional choices for this recipe, if available.

Chocolate Lavender Shortbread with Sea Salt

2 sticks (1 cup) unsalted butter, softened

2 tablespoons Lavender Honey (page 196, optional)

1 cup confectioners' sugar

1 teaspoon pure vanilla extract

⅔ cup cocoa powder

1½ cups all-purpose flour, plus more for rolling

1 tablespoon dried culinary lavender buds, ground

1 teaspoon kosher or coarse sea salt

Beat the butter and honey (if used) until creamy. Add the sugar and beat until fluffy. Add the vanilla, then beat in the cocoa powder on low speed. Add the flour, ground lavender buds, and salt to combine. The dough will be very soft. Divide the dough in half and place each half between two large sheets of parchment paper or plastic wrap. Roll out the dough to ¼ inch thick and transfer to two baking sheets. Refrigerate until firm, at least thirty minutes.

Preheat the oven to 350 degrees F (175 degrees C). Working with one piece of dough at a time, remove the top sheet of parchment and invert the dough onto a lightly floured work surface. Remove the second sheet of parchment. Using a floured 2-to-3-inch (5-to-7.5-cm) cookie cutter, stamp cookies as close together as possible. Transfer the cookies to parchment paper–lined baking sheets. Bake for twelve to fourteen minutes or until firm. Let cool on the baking sheets for ten minutes.

While the cookies are still warm, gently press a few flakes of sea salt into the top of each cookie. Transfer the cookies to a rack to cool completely. Reroll the scraps and cut out more cookies. Chill the scraps between batches if need be. When the cookies have cooled, lightly sprinkle them with powdered sugar.

EXTRACTS AND BITTERS

Typically, extracts are made with alcohol because it is a more efficient and quicker way to extract flavors from herbs and spices, as well as being easy and affordable, but you can make an extract without alcohol.

Lavender Extract

I always recommend using a good-quality 100 proof vodka for its neutral flavor or a rum or bourbon with 40-percent alcohol content.

¼ cup dried culinary lavender buds

1 cup vodka, rum, or bourbon (40 to 50 percent alcohol, which is 80 to 100 proof)

Gently press the dried lavender buds with a mortar and pestle to release the volatile oils. Place the crushed buds in a canning jar. Pour the alcohol over the buds and cap the jar. Shake well. Let it steep for three weeks at most, inverting the jar a few times per week. After three weeks, strain out the buds using a fine-mesh sieve or an unbleached coffee filter. To preserve the flavor, store in a dark glass bottle such as amber or cobalt.

Alcohol-Free Lavender Extract

Compared to making an extract with alcohol, the infusion process for nonalcoholic extract takes longer, and the shelf life for bitters made with glycerin is only one to two years.

3 tablespoons dried culinary lavender buds

¼ cup water

¾ cup food-grade vegetable glycerin

Combine the lavender buds (crushed with a mortar and pestle or not), water, and glycerin in a bottle and seal with a cap. Shake well. Store in a cool, dark place and allow to steep for four to six weeks. Shake the bottle once a week.

Lavender and Lemongrass Bitters

Bitters are botanicals, herbs, and roots infused into alcohol. They add a surprisingly rich flavor to beverages. Many bitters recipes make use of lemon and orange zest, two ingredients that pair well with lavender. This recipe achieves the citrus flavor by using fresh lemongrass, but fresh lemon zest can also be used. Adding dried gentian root (not powder) is optional. This bitter herb is found in many alcoholic beverages and helps tie flavors together. You can find it at a local herb shop or online.

Create your own cocktails by combining the bitters with any alcohol, like vodka, gin, or tequila. For a nonalcoholic drink, try lemonade, sparkling water, or tea. For a frozen treat, add to popsicles. Lavender bitters can also be used in baking: add to any recipe that calls for vanilla extract, along with or in place of the vanilla.

1 stalk fresh lemongrass

½ teaspoon dried gentian root (optional)

3 cardamom pods

6 anise or fennel seeds

3 tablespoons fresh lavender buds or 1 tablespoon dried culinary lavender buds

1 cup grain alcohol or high proof alcohol such as vodka, bourbon, or rum; or food-grade vegetable glycerin

Trim the root end from the lemongrass and discard. Trim 3 inches of the stalk starting from the trimmed end and slice crosswise as thin as possible. Combine the lemongrass, optional gentian root, cardamom pods, anise or fennel seeds, and lavender buds in a glass jar. Add the alcohol or glycerin and seal tightly. Shake vigorously for thirty seconds. Store in a cool, dark place for three weeks. Shake the jar every few days to promote infusion. Then strain the ingredients using a fine-mesh sieve and pour into an amber glass bottle with a dropper in the cap.

HERB AND SPICE MIXES

Ground lavender buds are a natural addition to herb and spice mixes. These mixes are a simple way to add a taste of lavender to savory dishes. Try the combinations I suggest here and then experiment with your own.

In small jars (clockwise from top): lavender lemon pepper, lavender chili spice mix, lavender rosemary salt. herbes de Provence, and lavender with rainbow peppercorns. Dried lavender buds (from left to right): 'Folgate', 'Croxton's Wild', 'Miss Katherine', 'Buena Vista', and 'Melissa'.

Lavender Chili Spice Mix

Add a hint of lavender to your chili. The lavender's spice notes marry well with hot chili peppers and linger in the background, making you guess what they could be. This versatile chili blend goes well with avocado fries or potato fries, or you can incorporate it in flour or breadcrumbs for dredging chicken.

For this blend, I like to use pink lavender like 'Miss Katherine' or 'Melissa' or 'Nana Alba' for their spicy note. I use a medium-spiced paprika chili powder, and I toast the cumin and coriander seeds to deepen their flavor by swirling for three to four minutes in a small heavy skillet over medium heat.

2 tablespoons cumin seeds, toasted

1 tablespoon coriander seeds, toasted

1 tablespoon dried culinary lavender buds

½ teaspoon salt

⅛ cup ground dried chili of your choice

Grind the seeds with the lavender buds and salt in a food processor or herb grinder. Add the ground chili and blend in the spice grinder once more until well mixed. Store in a sealed glass container.

Lavender Lemon Pepper

Lemon pepper made from scratch is a real treat. The lemon peels give a lemony flavor that really sings! I like using 'Buena Vista' lavender in this blend.

10 medium lemons, washed

2 tablespoons freshly ground black pepper

1 tablespoon granulated onion

2 teaspoons semi-coarse sea salt (optional)

1 teaspoon granulated garlic

1 teaspoon ground lavender buds

Preheat the oven to 200 degrees F (95 degrees C). Using a vegetable peeler, remove thin strips of lemon rind, avoiding the white pith. Line a baking sheet with parchment paper and lay the peels out on the sheet in a single layer so they do not touch each other. Bake for thirty to thirty-five minutes, until the sides begin to curl. Remove from the oven and allow to cool.

Grind the dried strips in a food processor, blender, or spice grinder for thirty seconds to one minute, depending on how chunky you want the result to be. In a bowl, stir together the dried lemon pieces, black pepper, granulated onion, optional sea salt, granulated garlic, and lavender buds. Store in an airtight container in a cool, dry place for up to three months.

Here are a few uses for lavender lemon pepper:

- Use as a dry rub or marinade for fish or chicken. For the marinade, whisk 3 tablespoons lavender lemon pepper with ¼ cup olive oil until well blended.
- Make a cheese spread by blending 1 to 2 teaspoons of lavender lemon pepper with ½ cup goat cheese or cream cheese.
- Sprinkle on popcorn or roasted potatoes.
- Season roasted asparagus. Drizzle one trimmed bunch of asparagus with olive oil and sprinkle with 1 teaspoon of lavender lemon pepper. Roast for eight minutes at 400 degrees F (200 degrees C), turning over once at four minutes. Add grated parmesan cheese for the last two minutes of roasting.

Insider tip: Don't let your lemon juice or rinds go to waste. Before you squeeze your lemons, peel the rind. Freeze freshly squeezed juice in ice cube trays for later use in meal preparation, baking, and beverages. Any leftover peeled and dried rinds can always be stored and used later in spice medleys and baking.

Herbes de Provence

Herbes de Provence is my all-time favorite spice blend, one I use in many dishes. For instance, for my mid-morning breakfast I often have an egg gathered fresh from the henhouse and either soft-boiled or fried and placed on top of avocado toast that has been drizzled with olive oil and sprinkled with herbes de Provence, salt, and freshly ground pepper, and garnished with sliced heirloom tomatoes from our vegetable garden.

There are many variations on herbes de Provence. Here is mine. I prefer to leave the fennel seeds and dried lavender buds whole so they stand out in appearance and add plenty of flavor. For the lavender buds, I like to use a dark-colored and floral cultivar such as 'Buena Vista', 'Wyckoff', or 'Royal Velvet'.

2 tablespoons dried Greek or Italian oregano

2 tablespoons dried sweet Italian basil

2 tablespoons crumbled whole dried sage leaves

1 teaspoon fennel seeds

1 teaspoon dried culinary lavender buds

In a bowl, combine the oregano, basil, sage leaves, fennel seeds, and lavender buds. Store in a glass jar with a tight-fitting lid.

Make a Snack from the Garden

This is among my favorite summer garden snacks.

Cherry Tomatoes with Goat Cheese, Olive Oil, and Herbes de Provence

2 cups (1 pint) cherry tomatoes, mixed colors

¼ cup goat cheese

2 tablespoons olive oil

2 teaspoons herbes de Provence

sea salt to taste

crackers

Slice the cherry tomatoes in half. Crumble the goat cheese over the tomatoes and drizzle with your favorite olive oil. Sprinkle with herbes de Provence and sea salt. Serve with crackers.

PEPPER MILL GRINDER RECIPES

I love to have a few spice grinders in my kitchen filled with different combinations of herbs and quality sea salt so that I can grind the spices right into or onto a dish. Of course, I use dried culinary lavender buds from my farm in the blends. Any blend can be used in a brine, lightly dusted over peaches and melons, ground onto steak or into clam chowder, sprinkled on popcorn, and even ground onto vanilla custard!

Pink Fusion Lavender Rainbow Salt

The warming and piquant quality of pepper produced by the pungent alkaloid piperine and its turpentine citrus flavors combines well with lavender's floral and spicy notes. I like to pair rainbow peppercorns with sea salts from Bolivia and Peru and dried buds from pink-flowered lavenders such as 'Miss Katherine', 'Melissa', and 'Hidcote Pink'. I suggest quantities of each ingredient here, but you can tailor this recipe to your liking. Let your taste buds be your guide.

¾ cup rainbow peppercorns

¼ cup pink coarse sea salt, such as Himalayan or Bolivian

1 tablespoon pink-flowered dried lavender buds

Combine the peppercorns, sea salt, and lavender buds in a bowl and transfer to a pepper mill.

Lavender Rosemary Salt

In this blend, the earthy, woodsy flavor of rosemary complements lavender's floral and mint notes. I prefer to use buds from 'Royal Velvet', 'Folgate', or 'Buena Vista' lavender along with French gray sea salt (*sel gris*), coarse grain, in this recipe. A grind of this is perfect for seasoning roasted vegetables like winter squash, onions, eggplant, mushrooms, carrots, and potatoes. You can also add it to fruits such as apricots, peaches, and plums, or pair it with chicken, lamb, or pork.

⅓ cup medium-to-coarse sea salt
1 tablespoon dried rosemary
1 teaspoon dried culinary lavender buds

Combine the sea salt, rosemary, and lavender buds in a bowl and transfer to a pepper mill.

Preserve Lemons with a Hint of Lavender

Lemons brined in a salty solution—in this recipe tinted pink by sprigs of lavender—become a silky-smooth umami-flavored ingredient that you can add to many dishes. You can use the entire lemon or just the rind, or you can scoop out the flesh and add it to enhance a vinaigrette, a pasta dish, cooked grains, stews, and main courses. Preserved lemon can also be given away as a gift. Buds of 'Folgate', 'Hidcote', or 'Royal Velvet' lavender work well in this recipe. You can use regular lemons or go with Meyer lemons, which are slightly sweet and less acidic.

Preserved Lemons with Lavender, Black Peppercorns, Star Anise, and Thyme

6–8 organic lemons, uncoated or well-scrubbed to remove any wax coating

6–8 tablespoons kosher salt

5–10 sprigs dried culinary lavender

2 sprigs dried thyme

10 black peppercorns

5 star anise pods

1 large dried red chili pepper (optional)

1 cup lemon juice, or enough to cover the lemons in the jar

Sterilize a quart jar by filling it with boiling water, letting the water sit for three minutes before pouring it out, and allowing the jar to dry without wiping it. Wash the lemons and cut a deep cross in each lemon all the way from the top to within 3/4 inch of the base. Be careful not to slice all the way through. Stuff each quartered lemon with 1 tablespoon of salt.

In the bottom of a large glass swing-top jar, place one tablespoon of salt. Using a muddler or a wooden spoon, push three lemons tightly together in the bottom of the jar. Gently incorporate the sprigs of lavender and thyme. Sprinkle peppercorns and anise pods throughout and add the optional chili pepper. Add a second layer of three to four more lemons. Press the lemons tightly into the jar. Add enough lemon juice to cover.

Close the jar and let it sit in a cool, dry place. You will notice juices beginning to accumulate. Shake the jar gently each day to distribute the salt and juices. After a week you can add more aromatic spices if you want, but be sure to add more lemon juice to cover the spices. Let the mixture ripen for thirty days before using. Rinse the preserved lemons under running water, as needed, before adding to a recipe. Preserved lemons will keep up to a year in the refrigerator.

Quartered lemons filled with kosher salt.

Here are some ideas for using preserved lemons:

- Chop the rind, pith, and/or flesh to your desired texture and combine in a vinaigrette.
- Mince and incorporate in avocado or pea mash for a salty-citrusy flavor.
- Combine lemon juice, lemon zest, and preserved lemon peel in a light cream sauce and toss with your favorite pasta.
- Add to roasted and buttered fingerling potatoes.
- Add to a bulgur wheat salad, a couscous salad, or any dish made with quinoa.
- Add to a relish or a creamy lemon dressing.
- Mix into a red lentil stew or soup.
- Give as a gift in an attractive swing-top jar, with a recipe that uses preserved lemon.

COMPOUND BUTTERS

Compound butter is the most versatile pantry item to keep on hand. You can store it in the freezer and slice it when you want to add a buttery, rich herb flavor to vegetables, meats, breads, and rice.

Compound butters are all made the same way. Begin with butter at room temperature (do not microwave to soften). In a mixing bowl, combine all the ingredients and stir until they are well distributed. Alternatively, you can add ingredients to a food processor and pulse until combined.

Lay out a piece of waxed paper and spoon the mixture into the lower center of the piece of paper. Fold the paper over the butter and roll the butter away from you to form a log shape. Twist each end of the paper and put the log in the freezer until firm, or refrigerate overnight. Once firm, the butter can be sliced into thin disks.

Here are three compound butter blends I love.

Herbed Compound Butter

Melt on a grilled steak, on fish or chicken, in pastas and mashed potatoes, or in potato soup. Spread on crusty sourdough bread or your favorite biscuit. Use as a cooking fat for eggs or omelets.

- 1 stick (½ cup) unsalted butter, softened to room temperature
- 1 tablespoon finely minced fresh thyme or rosemary
- 1 tablespoon finely minced shallot
- 1 teaspoon coarsely ground lavender buds or 1½ tablespoons finely minced fresh lavender flowers
- 1 teaspoon grated lemon zest
- ¼ teaspoon fine sea salt
- ¼ teaspoon ground black pepper

Spiced Compound Butter

Slather on corn on the cob or cornbread, baked sweet potato, salmon, or popcorn.

1 stick (½ cup) unsalted butter, softened to room temperature

2 teaspoons minced fresh lemon thyme or winter thyme, or ¼ teaspoon lime zest

1 teaspoon Lavender Chili Spice Mix (page 205)

¼ teaspoon sea salt

Sweet Compound Butter

Melt on pork chops, spread on cornbread, or mash into freshly baked sweet potatoes.

1 stick (½ cup) unsalted butter, softened to room temperature

2 tablespoons Lavender Honey (page 196)

1 teaspoon finely chopped rosemary

1 teaspoon finely chopped sage

½ teaspoon minced orange rind

¼ teaspoon sea salt

Chapter 7

Seasonal Crafts

Nature's offerings and a love for lavender inspire craft making and gift giving throughout the seasons. The most rewarding part of growing plants is having a bountiful garden to share with people you care about. You can also adorn your home inside and out and nourish your body with healing plants. Lavender has so much to offer the crafter.

Autumn Home Decor

Along with drying lavender throughout the summer season, I dry other flowers I grow. That way, I always have an abundant supply of material to make wreaths, bouquets, and swags, beautiful autumn arrangements I use to adorn my home. Dried purple lavender flowers add an unexpected pop of color to the brown, yellow, and orange hues of fall and impart a pleasant scent wherever you place your arrangement.

I have discovered the flowers that dry best and maintain their vibrant colors. Throughout the summer season, I harvest strawflowers, celosias, zinnias, amaranth, broom corns, grasses, chili peppers, and herbs. Before the first frost arrives, I gather the last of the flowering lavender, grasses, and flowers like marigolds and statice. I use these flowers and the ones I gathered during summer to decorate my home for the fall and winter season. It brings me joy to celebrate the incoming season by using what nature has to offer and what my garden provides before it is put to rest for winter.

Autumn arrangements using dried lavender and flowers adorn our shop in Palisade, Colorado.

216 LAVENDER FOR ALL SEASONS

An Autumn Door Swag

I like to combine lavender, dried late-summer flowers, and dried peppers to make a door swag—what I call an upside-down flower bouquet. Late-summer flowers that can easily be dried are marigolds, double-blooming lavender cultivars like 'Forever Blue', 'Lavang 21', 'Buena Vista', and blooming 'Impress Purple' or 'Riverina Thomas'. Dried corn stalks, pampas grasses, chili peppers, and broom corn are also great additions to fill in arrangements. Whatever you fancy! Lavender flowers, especially in blue-violet, white, and pink, pop with fall-colored flowers. You can also make a swag using fresh flowers. The method is the same whether dried or fresh. If you do use fresh flowers, be sure to go back once the flowers have dried and tighten the wire to secure the stems in place, since the stems shrink as they dry.

dried lavender bundles

dried flowers and other plant material, six to eight different types

wired ribbon, two to three colors

scissors

18-inch fabric-wrapped 22-gauge stem wire for securing ribbons

18-inch fabric-wrapped 20-gauge stem wire for bundling stems

needle-nose pliers

thick twine or rope-wrapped wire to make a hanging loop

hot glue gun and hot glue stick

hand pruners

Note that for the fabric-wrapped stem wire, green or brown wrap works. The higher the gauge of the wire, the thinner the wire is; the lower the gauge, the thicker the wire. For wreaths, use 20- and 22-gauge wire. These are easier to bend but still sturdy.

Materials for autumn swag.

SEASONAL CRAFTS

1. Choose the plant materials you want to use. Remove unwanted lower leaves before you start arranging. Combine the colors the way you want them and arrange in a loosely organized fashion so that you can pick up the materials easily. Plan to place longer-stemmed materials, like grasses and corn, toward the back of the swag.

2. Choose your ribbon. Combine ribbons of different widths in colors that will bring out your flower colors, or keep it simple with a single ribbon. Prepare your ribbon(s) by looping into bows and layering one on top of the other if you are using more than one ribbon, with the option of layering a third ribbon.

3. Wire your bows together with 22-gauge stem wire. Secure by twisting the wire at the back of the final bow. Leave the wire long enough at both ends to wrap around your bundle of plant materials.

4. Arrange your plant materials in layers, leaving longer stems in the back and shorter stems toward the front. For a large swag, make three to four layers of material; for a smaller swag, two layers of material. Fan the bottom flowers, and as you work your way up, narrow the fan.

5. Once the materials are arranged, wire the stems together using 20-gauge stem wire. Twist the wire behind the arrangement and tighten with needle-nose pliers.

6. Attach the bow to the arrangement by placing the bow on the table face-down with the extra wire extending out on both sides, then placing the plant bundle face-down on top of the bow and encircling the bundle with the wire. Twist the wire and tighten with needle-nose pliers to ensure nothing comes loose.

7. Wrap thick twine or rope-wrapped wire around the bundle to make a hanging loop.

Choose your dried plant materials. Here, emerald green amaranth, large orange marigolds, common sage, three types of lavender ('Buena Vista', 'Edelweiss', 'Riverina Thomas'), broom corn, wheat, yarrow, wild marjoram, cayenne chili peppers, orange zinnias, and craspedia.

Get your ribbon bows ready.

Wire your bow using 22-gauge stem wire.

Arrange your plant materials in layers.

Wire your stems together.

Attach the bow from the back of the swag.

Make a hanger for the swag.

SEASONAL CRAFTS

8. Dress the top of the swag (the stem end) with additional stems of lavender and plant material. Cut the stems short and hot-glue them above the bow. Secure both by using hot glue and tying wire around the stems to ensure they don't come apart.

9. Using hand pruners, trim the stems to the desired length. Position ribbon and loops where you want them and hang the swag in your home, on your front door, or on an entry gate.

Insert additional plant material—shown here, dried chili peppers, lavender, sage, and broom corn—at the top of the swag above the bow.

Trim the stems to your desired length.

Hang your creation to enjoy.

Variation: this large swag has three layers of plant materials plus dried marigold and yarrow flowers hot-glued to the middle of the bow.

Winter Balms and Sweet-Smelling Gifts

Winter is a time to slow down, take care of yourself, and create some heartfelt gifts for the ones you love. Nourishing balms and salves crafted with lavender essential oil are two of my favorite offerings to share during the holidays. For myself, in the morning, I moisturize dry, well-worn hands with the healing hydration of lavender-scented balms. In the evening when I get ready for bed, scents of lavender and eucalyptus set the tone for a good night's sleep.

Tins of lavender-peppermint balm ready for enjoying or gifting.

Before using essential oils topically, perform a small patch test on your inner forearm or back by applying a small quantity of diluted essential oil. Cover with a waterproof bandage and monitor for any skin irritation such as swelling, itching, or redness. Wash the area if you experience any irritation. If no irritation occurs after forty-eight hours, it is safe to use on your skin.

SEASONAL CRAFTS

Bases for Balms, Perfumes, and Massage Oils

When you make balms, perfumes, and massage oils, you will want to dilute your lavender essential oil with a high-quality carrier oil. Seed and nut oils such as apricot kernel oil, jojoba oil, extra virgin olive oil, grapeseed oil, and coconut oil are nutrient-rich and have high levels of vitamins A, E, and F. Whenever possible, use organic oils.

- APRICOT KERNEL OIL is derived from the kernel of the apricot (*Prunus armeniaca*). It has properties similar to almond oil, being odorless and light in weight, texture, and color.

- COCONUT OIL comes from the fruit of the coconut palm (*Cocos nucifera*). Fractionated oil from the coconut palm is odorless and remains liquid at room temperature, and it is also clear, lightweight, and nongreasy. I prefer to use unrefined organic coconut oil because it is minimally processed and is the most nourishing for your skin, although it does have a mild scent. Avoid refined coconut oil as the high-temperature refining process removes many of coconut oil's antioxidants.

- EXTRA VIRGIN OLIVE OIL comes from pressing the fruit of the olive tree (*Olea europaea*). It is a moderately heavy base oil, high in beneficial vitamins and minerals. Blended extra virgin olive oil can be lighter in weight and is odorless. I like to combine olive oil and refined coconut oil to balance the two, while maximizing the skin benefit of both oils. Or for a simple yet nourishing balm, blend it with beeswax.

- GRAPESEED OIL is a by-product of making wine from grapes (*Vitis vinifera*). For cosmetic and skin care purposes, use cold-pressed grapeseed oil. It is lightweight, is easily absorbed by the skin, and has a neutral scent. Cold-pressed grapeseed oil is known to contain high levels of fatty acids and vitamin E.

- JOJOBA OIL is derived from pressed seeds of the jojoba shrub (*Simmondsia chinensis*). A medium-weight base oil, it penetrates the skin well and leaves no oily residue. It does not turn rancid, though it does need refrigeration. It blends well with essential oils and has a good shelf life.

As with any natural ingredient, always start with a spot test to ensure a carrier oil works for your skin type. Negative reactions can occur in highly sensitive skin.

When diluting essential oils in a carrier oil, always start with a low dilution ratio like 1 percent (1 drop of essential oil per 100 drops of carrier oil) and then increase to the dilution ratio desired. For leave-on body products such as balms, a 2-percent dilution ratio is the recommended upper limit. A safe and effective rule of thumb is to use 2 drops of essential oil per 98 drops of carrier oil, or about 10 to 12 drops per ounce.

Peppermint Lavender Balm

The simple combination of lavender and peppermint soothes skin and relieves sinus congestion. Perfect as a winter gift. These instructions make eight to ten 1-ounce containers or sixteen to twenty ½-ounce containers.

- **4-cup Pyrex measuring cup**
- **plastic measuring spoons and cups**
- **wooden skewers to use as stirrers**
- **parchment paper**
- **10 1-ounce containers or 20 ½-ounce containers**
- **½ cup cold-pressed organic grapeseed oil (or substitute apricot kernel oil, extra virgin olive oil, or jojoba oil)**
- **¼ cup unrefined organic coconut oil, fractionated if you do not like coconut scent**
- **¼ cup pure unrefined, unbleached beeswax (beads are my preference as they dissolve quickly and evenly)**
- **1 teaspoon organic 5000 IU vitamin E oil**
- **½ teaspoon 100% pure lavender essential oil (from *Lavandula angustifolia* for a floral note, from *L. ×intermedia* for a bright and herbaceous note)**
- **½ teaspoon 100% pure peppermint (*Mentha piperita*) essential oil**

Materials for peppermint lavender balm.

SEASONAL CRAFTS

1. In your 4-cup Pyrex measuring cup, combine the grapeseed oil, coconut oil, and beeswax.

2. Heat the ingredients in a nonreactive double boiler to avoid direct heat. If you do not have a nonreactive double boiler, you can use the Pyrex measuring cup in a pan of boiling water to create the same effect. Stir constantly with a wooden stir stick until all the ingredients are melted. Remove from heat. This will ensure a creamy texture.

Combine the carrier ingredients.

Fill the measuring cup right to the brim for a perfect measurement.

Heat the ingredients in a double boiler, or in a Pyrex measuring cup in a pan of boiling water, until melted.

3. Vigorously stir in the vitamin E oil and essential oils. Test for the strength of the essential oils by placing a dot of melted balm on your hand. Rub into your skin and smell the fragrance. If you need to adjust upward, add only a drop of essential oil at a time.

4. Set out your tins on parchment paper. Pour the melted mixture up to the upper ring of the 1- ounce tin. Be quick, as the liquid solidifies fast as it cools.

5. Let the balm sit for ten minutes to solidify, then cap with the lid.

Add the essential oils to the melted base ingredients.

Pour the liquid balm into tins.

Cool and cap the balm.

SEASONAL CRAFTS   225

Winter Solstice Balm

This balm contains the warming and uplifting aromas of winter: the spice of ginger and the sweet scents of orange and lavender. It's just what you and your loved ones need to stay grounded and calm through the holidays. Makes eight to ten 1-ounce containers or sixteen to twenty ½-ounce containers.

You should never use essential oils undiluted in eyes or on mucus membranes, and you should not take them internally unless working with a qualified expert practitioner. Keep them away from children. Long-term overexposure can cause some people to develop a sensitivity to lavender.

4-cup Pyrex measuring cup

plastic measuring spoons and cups

wooden skewers to use as stirrers

parchment paper

10 1-ounce containers or 20 ½-ounce containers

⅓ cup pure unrefined, unbleached beeswax (beads are my preference as they dissolve quickly and evenly)

¼ cup unrefined organic coconut oil, fractionated if you do not like coconut scent

¼ cup + 3 tablespoons cold-pressed organic grapeseed oil (or substitute apricot kernel oil, extra virgin olive oil, or jojoba oil)

3 tablespoons organic apricot kernel oil

1 teaspoon + ¼ teaspoon organic 5000 IU vitamin E oil

½ teaspoon 100% pure essential oil of true lavender (*Lavandula angustifolia*)

½ teaspoon 100% pure essential oil of sweet orange (*Citrus sinensis*)

¼ teaspoon 100% pure essential oil of ginger (*Zingiber officinale*)

Follow the same method as for the Peppermint Lavender Balm on pages 223–225.

Measuring Essential Oils

Recipes that call for essential oils often use measurements in drops for smaller quantities and measuring spoons for larger quantities. I like to use pipettes when adding drops to a recipe, as this tends to be more precise than using the essential oil dripper insert. The volume of a given number of drops of essential oil can vary depending on the viscosity of the oil and the orifice of the dropper. The table gives approximate equivalencies for measuring lavender essential oil, but note that these quantities should be considered estimates only. Not all essential oil drops are equal.

APPROXIMATE EQUIVALENCIES FOR LAVENDER ESSENTIAL OIL

Drops	Milliliters	Teaspoons	Ounces	Drams or cups
6	.3 ml	.06 tsp		
10	about ½ ml	⅒ tsp	.5 oz	
12	about ⅝ ml	⅛ tsp	.6 oz	
20	1 ml	.2 tsp	1/12 oz	¼ dram
25	1¼ ml	¼ tsp	1.25	⅓ dram
50	2½ ml	½ tsp	2.5	⅔ dram
100	about 5 ml	1 tsp	⅙ oz	1⅓ dram
150	about 13.5 ml	1½ tsp	¼ oz	2 drams
300	about 15 ml	3 tsp	½ oz	4 drams
600	about 30 ml	6 tsp	1 oz	8 drams
	60 ml	12 tsp	2 oz	16 drams
	120 ml	24 tsp	4 oz	½ cup
	237 ml	48 tsp	8 oz	1 cup
	473 ml	98 tsp	16 oz	2 cups

Closet Sachet

A sachet filled with lavender buds from your garden makes a very special gift, whether you fill a premade linen or organza fabric bag or sew a unique pouch yourself. It can be hung from a hanger and keeps your winter coats and closet smelling fresh. It is a healthy alternative to mothballs with a scent that lasts for years. To get more aroma, lightly pinch the sachet between your fingers to release the oils in the buds.

I love the design of this closet sachet. It can be sewn by hand or using a sewing machine with a buttonhole foot. A seam ripper comes in handy, too. I like using linen fabric and a velvet ribbon to add a touch of elegance. The finished sachet is 7 inches high by 4¾ inches wide.

a piece of pretty fabric measuring at least 8 × 8½ inches

an 8-inch length of sheer ribbon at least 2 inches wide, preferably in a light color

a 15-inch length of ¼-inch or ⅝-inch velvet ribbon to make a bow

cotton thread to match the fabric

¾ cup to 1 cup dried lavandin buds

hot glue gun and hot glue stick

scissors

1. Make a pattern by cutting a piece of paper to measure 8 × 8½ inches. Cut the fabric to the pattern.

2. Cut the 8-inch length of sheer ribbon to 2 inches wide. Pin one long edge of the ribbon to one 8-inch-long edge of the fabric with right sides together, and sew along the edge, leaving a ¼-inch seam allowance. Then pin the other long edge of the ribbon to the other 8-inch-long edge of the fabric with right sides together, and sew along the edge, again leaving a ¼-inch seam allowance. Center the strip of ribbon vertically and iron the pouch flat, with both seams toward the fabric.

3. At the upper corners, draw and sew a diagonal seam. Then sew straight across the top of the bag, leaving a ¼-inch seam allowance. Trim the extra fabric from the corners, leaving a ¼-inch margin.

4. Turn the bag right side out. Starting ¾ inch from the top of the sachet, sew through both layers to make a vertical buttonhole 1 inch long. On a sewing machine, use the buttonhole foot to make the buttonhole and then cut the buttonhole open using a seam ripper. If sewing by hand, cut a 1-inch opening and then use a buttonhole stitch to finish.

5. Fill the sachet with lavandin buds. Then sew the bottom shut by hand using a slip stitch. Tie the velvet ribbon into a bow and hot glue or sew the bow above the buttonhole, near the upper seam.

Voilà! Slip the sachet over a clothes hanger and hang it in your closet.

Materials for lavender closet sachet.

Make a paper pattern and cut your fabric.

Sew the ribbon to the fabric and center the ribbon vertically, then iron the pouch flat.

Fill the sachet with lavardin buds and sew the bottom seam shut.

The finished sachet, slipped over a clothes hanger.

Spring Cleaning with Lavender

Spring is the time to throw open the windows and sweep out the dust and cobwebs. I clean my entire house with lavender essential oil and hydrosol, the floral water left after the essential oil distillation process. The terpene compounds are just enough to clean surfaces gently. I like to add a few drops of sweet orange for a citrusy aroma that lifts mood and reduces stress.

All-Purpose Lavender Cleaner

I clean my countertops, wood, and tile floors using this lavender cleaner. I have found that lavandin hydrosol works the best on grime and leaves a shiny, clean surface. When I am done, my home smells fresh and soothing, unlike the scent left behind when harsh chemicals are used.

2 cups distilled water, or lavender or lavandin hydrosol

¼ cup white vinegar

12 drops 100% pure lavender or lavandin essential oil

8 drops 100% pure sweet orange (*Citrus sinensis*) essential oil

optional: 1 teaspoon castile (mild option) or phosphorous-free dish soap, or washing soda (sodium carbonate works as a stronger cleaner)

Fill a clean spray bottle with the distilled water or hydrosol. Add the vinegar, essential oils, and optional soap or washing soda, and shake well.

Spring cleaning with lavandin essential oil and lavandin hydrosol.

My All-Purpose, No-Rinse Floor Cleaner

This cleaner can be used on tile, linoleum, and wood floors alike. Use more hydrosol in the mix for very dirty floors. If you do not have hydrosol, you can use 15 to 20 drops of lavender or lavandin essential oil.

1 gallon warm water
½ cup white vinegar (optional)
1–2 cups lavandin hydrosol

Combine the ingredients in a bucket and stir well.

Nothing goes to waste at my house. When I am done cleaning the floors, I pour the used water from the bucket into toilet bowls, then scrub and flush.

Lavender Dryer Bags

Lavender dryer bags are a natural antistatic laundry deodorizer. Besides using them in your dryer, you can use them in your bathwater, closets, and dresser drawers to add a refreshing scent. A high-camphor lavandin cultivar like 'Grosso', 'Impress Purple', 'Gros Bleu', or 'Riverina Thomas' works best.

5 large press-and-seal unbleached teabags
(find at your natural food grocer or online)
1 cup dried lavandin buds

Scoop 3 tablespoons of buds into each bag. Iron the open seam on the highest setting to seal the bags. To ensure a good seal, iron each side of the bag.

Alternative: If you do not have buds, you can use lavandin essential oil and wool dryer balls. Drop 10 to 12 drops of essential oil on the ball and throw it into your dryer. One wool ball can last for up to a thousand dryer cycles!

LAVENDER FOR DOG CARE

You have to be careful when using essential oil around pets; lavender is not safe for birds or many small animals, such as cats. For dogs, lavender can be used to calm nerves and enhance skin care, but it can cause irritation and distress if misused. Be mindful of your dog's acute sense of smell and use a less concentrated solution than you would for humans.

There are hundreds of homemade dog shampoo and deodorizer recipes. These recipes incorporate lavender for its calming and soothing qualities. Vinegar deodorizes and adds shine. Castile soap helps bind the ingredients together, and baking soda balances the acidity of vinegar and water, which is pH neutral.

Our farm dog, Lizzy, looks a little skeptical, but relaxed.

Gentle Dog Shampoo

Dogs have sensitive skin, and it is important to use a shampoo that does not strip away their natural oils. This simple recipe adapted from the American Kennel Club incorporates lavender to relieve itchy skin and calm anxiety.

¼ cup dish soap formulated for sensitive skin and free of fragrance, colors, and dyes

3 drops 100% pure lavender essential oil

2 cups warm water

½ cup white vinegar

First combine the dish soap and essential oil in a spray bottle and shake well. Then add the water and vinegar and shake vigorously once again. Wet your dog's coat with warm water and spray with the shampoo, avoiding the eyes. Work the shampoo into the coat, creating a thick lather. Rinse thoroughly and repeatedly, even if you think all signs of shampoo are gone.

Dog Deodorizer and Calming Spray

Diluted lavender oil is generally considered safe for topical use on dogs. A light dilution makes this spray safe and easy to make.

1 tablespoon castile soap

2–4 drops 100 % pure lavender essential oil

1 tablespoon white vinegar

pinch of baking soda or coarse sea salt

4 ounces distilled water, or 2 ounces distilled water mixed with 2 ounces lavender hydrosol

First combine the soap and essential oil in a small glass measuring cup, and mix well. Then add the vinegar and salt, and mix well. Pour into an 8-ounce spray bottle. Add the distilled water or water-hydrosol solution. Cap and shake to combine. Cover the face and eyes of your dog and spray onto the coat to get rid of odor and calm nerves.

Lavender Hydrosol and Its Many Uses

Over the years, essential oils and their many uses have become better known. Even though the art of distilling hydrosols has been around for a millennium, awareness of hydrosol's benefits and uses is just dawning in today's public eye. Many lavender growers sell not only their lavender essential oil but also their hydrosols. You may see hydrosol sprays for sale in bath and body stores, on mail-order websites, and in natural markets. If you have access, ordering directly from an experienced and reputable distiller-producer is best. Reach out to your local lavender farmer to inquire what they may have.

I have the good fortune to have access to lavender hydrosol 365 days a year, since I distill hundreds of pounds of lavender and other herbs every growing season. The more I distill lavender hydrosol, the more I appreciate its benefits and how many applications there are. These fragrant waters are packed with beneficial hydrophilic (water-soluble) compounds present in lavender but not present in the essential oil, along with trace amounts of non-water-soluble compounds. I have come to rely on it more than I do my essential oils, as the compounds in hydrosol are gentle enough to use where an essential oil would be irritating to a particular skin type or condition.

Do not expect the smell of hydrosol to be similar to lavender or lavandin essential oil. The smell is slightly floral, more grassy and herbaceous. For some it may be a scent that takes getting accustomed to. It is important to store hydrosol in clear glass so you can see if any contaminants develop—particulates or blooms such as molds.

I keep it in half-gallon jars and cannot imagine living without it. You may be thinking, What in the world would I do with a half gallon of lavender hydrosol? My answer is, just about anything. Like white vinegar, baking soda, and coconut oil, lavender hydrosol is one of those go-to products that never fails. Lavender hydrosol holds its own against synthetic home and body products, providing a natural alternative to many conventional items. Here are some of my favorite applications:

- Wipe counters and floors. I love to mix lavandin hydrosol with white vinegar to use as a floor cleaner. The blend picks up spills and dirt while acting as a disinfectant.

- Soften your clothes. Where you would add fabric softener in your washer, add hydrosol instead. It does a fantastic job of softening clothes and ridding them of musty smells. Lavender hydrosol imparts a crisp, clean aroma and leaves clothes smelling fresh.

- Clean your car's interior. Lavandin is a very effective cleaner, due to its high terpene compounds. Lavandin hydrosol cleans both hard surfaces and fabric surfaces, making it a great option for cleaning the inside of your car. With the same water-soluble compounds and the same antibacterial and antifungal properties as lavandin essential oil, lavandin hydrosol helps get rid of the germs and sticky messes that build up in our car interiors, leaving behind a sweet, subtle aroma. Bottle hydrosol in a mist spray bottle and apply it to any surface you'd like to clean.

- Create your own bath and body products. Lavender hydrosol can be a valuable addition to any beauty regimen as a base for homemade facial cleansers, salves, and hair and skin toner. It is mildly astringent but not drying, and it balances all skin types. It also soothes sunburns and skin irritations.

- Take luxurious baths with lavender hydrosol and bath salts to create a spa experience right at home. Hydrosol has a softening effect in water. It gives an earthy smoothness that feels both revitalizing and soothing to the skin.

- Clean cuts on people and pets. Lavandin hydrosol is gentle but holds all the healing power of lavender. Use hydrosol to clean minor scrapes and soothe rashes and bug bites.

- Use as a calming spray for kids and adults alike. Put hydrosol in a spritzer spray bottle and use as needed.

- Make a lavender hydrosol compress. You can place it on the neck, shoulders, or forehead to relieve headaches, tension, and stress. As a standard practice, after I am done filtering the hydrosols into sterilized glass jars, I wring out the filter and place it on my neck and forehead. I am instantly reminded why I love to grow and process lavender.

- Make delicious drinks and desserts. From cocktails to infused waters, hydrosol adds a refreshing and interesting flavor to drinks. Use just ¼ teaspoon per pint, as a little goes a long way. Cooking with lavender hydrosol is also a great way to infuse your foods with the taste of lavender. I like to add it to my cherry jam along with lavender simple syrup.

- Lavender hydrosol is quite stable if kept at a constant temperature without fluctuations. It can last up to two years if stored in the refrigerator in a sterilized glass jar, although the scent tends to degrade after eighteen months. I like to use mine within twelve months.

A half-gallon jar of hydrosol made with fresh *Lavandula angustifolia* 'Maillette' can be used to fill a sprayer bottle kept ready for a variety of uses.

Fresh Summer Wreaths

Summer is the best time to make fresh lavender wreaths, bouquets, and floral crowns or halos. Working with fresh lavender is easier than using dried lavender because fresh lavender is more pliable, and you use less product. You can use either lavandin or true lavender for fresh creations. I like using cultivars like 'Betty's Blue', 'Lavang 21', 'Impress Purple', or 'Riverina Thomas' for a lighter purple color. 'Provence' and 'Super' are easy to work with, as well.

A Lavender Wreath

There are many styles of wreaths and methods for making them. The one I share here has a uniform look and holds up well over time. I will demonstrate a few simple tricks to secure the lavender once it has dried on the wreath form. This method of making the wreath's form and attaching stems can be used to make a variety of different styles. The wreath form comes in handy for other projects, too.

2 large bundles of fresh lavender

wrapped 22-gauge stem wire for making the form

26-gauge floral paddle wire for tying lavender to the form

½-inch to 1-inch ribbon

piece of cardboard to draw pattern on

micro-tip pruners

scissors

needle nose pliers

tape measure

felt tip pen

Materials to create fresh lavender wreaths.

LAVENDER FOR ALL SEASONS

Completed lavender wreath.

1. Make the wreath form by first looping the wrapped wire twice to form a circle measuring 8 inches in diameter and then wrapping the wire around the double loop to secure it. Cut the wire and tuck the end into the form so it does not stick out.

Loop the wrapped wire to make an 8-inch wreath form.

2. Use a piece of cardboard to make a pattern showing how wide the finished wreath will be. Trace your wreath form onto the cardboard with a felt tip pen. Measure 4 inches or more from this circle to make an outer circle; the farther out you make your outer circle, the wider the finished wreath will be. Your lavender sprigs will not extend beyond this outer edge. To make a perfect circle, trace the bottom of a plate or bucket.

3. Anchor your 26-gauge paddle wire to the wreath form by looping the wire through a couple of strands of wrapped wire on the form and securing by twisting the paddle wire eight to ten times. Now you are ready to begin adding fresh lavender to the form.

4. If needed, trim the lavender stems so that 5 to 6 inches of stem remain below the flowers.

5. Attach approximately six stems of lavender at one time by holding them in place on the wreath form and looping the paddle wire twice around the stems at the base of the flowers.

Make a wreath pattern using cardboard and a felt tip pen.

Anchor the paddle wire to the wreath form.

Trim the ends of the lavender stems.

Wire six stems to the form at one time.

6. Trim the stems, leaving 2 inches below the flowers. Take another six flower stems and overlap them on the exposed stems of the attached flowers. Wrap the paddle wire twice around the stems. Repeat this all the way around the wreath form. To maintain an even shape, be sure the stems do not extend beyond the outer circle of your pattern.

7. When you attach the last bunch of lavender, hide the stems by tucking them under the first bunch of lavender you attached.

8. To finish off the wreath, cut the paddle wire leaving an 8-inch tail. Thread this tail in and out of the wreath form two to three times to secure, and cut off any excess wire. Attach a hanger by looping a ribbon through the wreath form.

9. An important last step is to tighten the paddle wire from the back. Using needle nose pliers, grab the wire and gently twist. Do not twist too hard or you might snap the stems. Once the lavender has completely dried, tighten the wires again the same way to prevent the lavender from falling out.

Variations: For depth and texture, you could use lavender of two or three different colors, or you could alternate lavender with fresh flowers or herbs from your garden that dry well, such as sage, wild marjoram, thyme, yarrow, celosia, and amaranth.

Trim the stems, leaving 2 inches below the flowers.

Keep wiring bunches of lavender to the wreath form, staying within the outer circle on the cardboard.

Tuck the stems of the last bunch under the first bunch.

Cut the paddle wire and thread through the wreath form to secure the end.

Tighten the wire.

SEASONAL CRAFTS   241

A Fresh Flower Halo

A lavender crown, or *corona de lavanda*, is such a fun and magical piece to make. Three sisters who have worked on the farm with me for years used to braid marigolds together in Mexico. When our marigolds bloomed here on the farm, they showed me how to do it. One day a bride wanted to take pictures on the farm and asked if we could make her a fresh halo that she could wear in her hair. The sisters used their braided marigold method to make a halo using fresh lavender.

Every summer, we get giddy and let our creative juices flow when we have time to make these gorgeous fresh lavender halos. We sport the floral halos on our brimmed hats or wear them in our hair. These halos are among the best ways to showcase the beauty of lavender in bloom, and they can be adorned with other flowers that happen to be blooming in the garden. They are easy to make once you get the hang of it and bring so much joy!

2 fresh lavender bundles
26-gauge floral paddle wire
ribbon of your choice

Completed halo adorned with fresh coneflowers.

242   LAVENDER FOR ALL SEASONS

1. Organize your lavender stems by grouping six together and lining up the groups side by side. Leave the stems long because you will be braiding them.

2. Start with two groups, one held in each hand with stems pointing down and flowers pointing up. Cross the stems of the group held in the right hand over the stems in your left hand just where the flowers begin on each stem. Fold the stems held in your right hand over the stems in your left hand and upward so the righthand stems now point up, in between the two groups of flowers. Then fold the righthand stems over the lefthand stems again to point down, and consolidate them with the other stems, firmly holding with the left hand the place where the stems intersect.

3. Add a third group by holding it flowers-up in the right hand, placing it at the point where the stems intersect, and folding the stems up and over as you did with the first two groups. Consolidate them with the other stems and hold firmly.

Organize groups of stems. Here, 'Edelweiss' and 'Impress Purple' are mixed in each group.

Begin the braid with a group of lavender held in each hand and cross the group to the right over the group to the left.

Add a third group and consolidate the stems.

SEASONAL CRAFTS   243

4. Continue adding groups and braiding until you get to the desired length. Measure around the crown of your favorite hat or your head to determine this length.

5. To secure stem ends, loop the floral wire around one end of the braid and tie a knot, leaving 8 inches of excess wire. Cross the two ends of the braid over each other and wrap the floral wire around the stems four to five times. Enhance your halo by attaching flowers or ribbon.

When the lavender halo dries, it will still look beautiful on your hat. You can also remove the halo from your hat and use it to adorn your walls. At our farm, we have collected these halos throughout the summers and they have ended up decorating our shop walls—a beautiful reminder of past harvests.

Continue braiding, adding one group at a time.

Measure the braid to match the circumference of your hat's crown.

Tie off one end of the braided lavender with floral wire and then wire the two ends of the braid together.

Decorate the halo with a ribbon or adorn with fresh flowers like the yarrow and gomphrena shown here.

Ella celebrates lavender by adorning her sun hat!

A halo with a ribbon can double as a wreath.

SEASONAL CRAFTS 245

Sources and Resources

BIBLIOGRAPHY AND FURTHER READING

The National Center for Biotechnology Information of the National Library of Medicine makes available an extensive library of worldwide research about various species of *Lavandula*. Go to ncbi.nlm.nih.gov and enter "lavender" into the search box.

Bader, Sarah Berringer. 2012. *The Lavender Lover's Handbook*. Portland, OR: Timber Press.

Bayton, Dr. Ross, and Richard Sneesby. 2019. *RHS Colour Companion: A Visual Dictionary of Colour for Gardeners*. London: Mitchell Beazley.

Briscione, James, with Brooke Parkhurst. 2018. *The Flavor Matrix: The Art and Science of Pairing Common Ingredients to Create Extraordinary Dishes*. Boston: Harvest.

Crisan, Ioana, et al. 2023. "Current Trends for Lavender (*Lavandula angustifolia* Mill.) Crops and Products with Emphasis on Essential Oil Quality," *Plants* 12(2).

Dlugos, Daniel. 2022. *Distribution and Management of Phytophthora Species on Lavender in the United States*. Clemson University, *All Dissertations*, tigerprints. clemson.edu/all_dissertations/3134.

Dlugos, Daniel, William Bridges, and Steven Jeffers. 2024. "Phytophthora Root and Crown Rot of Lavender: New Host-Pathogen Relationships Involving Six Species of Phytophthora and Three Species of Lavandula," *Plant Disease* 108(3).

Guo, Xiangyang, and Pu Wang. 2020. "Aroma Characteristics of Lavender Extract and Essential Oil from *Lavandula angustifolia* Mill.," *Molecules* 25(23).

Harman, Ann. 2023. *Harvest to Hydrosol: Distill Your Own Exquisite Hydrosols at Home*. 2nd ed. Fruitland, WA: Iag Botanics.

Hawke, Richard G. 2017. "Lavender for Northern Gardens," Chicago Botanic Garden *Plant Evaluation Notes* 42.

Hoffman, David. 2003. *Medical Herbalism: The Science and Practice of Herbal Medicine*. Rochester, VT: Healing Arts Press.

Lafferty, Lida. 2016. *Spike It with Lavender: Recipes for Living*. Palisade, CO: Lavender Association of Colorado.

Lis-Balchin, Maria, ed. 2002. *Lavender: The Genus Lavandula*. London: CRC Press.

McGimpsy, J. A., and N. G. Porter. 1999. *Lavender: A Grower's Guide for Commercial Production*. New Zealand Institute for Crop and Food Research.

McNaughton, Virginia. 2010. *Lavender: The Grower's Guide*. 2nd ed. Portland, OR: Timber Press.

Rose, Jeanne. 1999. *375 Essential Oils and Hydrosols*. Berkeley, CA: North Atlantic Books.

Shipley, Sharon. 2004. *The Lavender Cookbook*. Philadelphia, PA: Running Press.

Tucker, Arthur, and Thomas Debaggio. 2009. *The Encyclopedia of Herbs: A Comprehensive Reference to Herbs of Flavor and Fragrance*. Portland, OR: Timber Press.

Upson, Tim, and Susyn Andrews. 2004. *The Genus Lavandula*. Portland, OR: Timber Press.

Valchev, Hristo, et al. 2022. "Pollinators of *Lavandula angustifolia* Mill., an Important Factor for Optimal Production of Lavender Essential Oil," *BioRisk* 17(1).

MAIL ORDER LAVENDER PLANT COMPANIES

Charsaw Farms (Goodwin Creek Gardens)
charsawfarms.com
Located in Napa, California, and Williams, Oregon. Large retail selection of lavender plants and other herbs and perennials.

High Country Gardens
highcountrygardens.com
Specializes in western gardens and xeriscape plants. Comprehensive retail selection of lavender plants.

Mountain Valley Growers
mountainvalleygrowers.com
Specializes in herbs, vegetables and fruits, roses, and lavender. Offers retail and wholesale.

Peace Tree Farm
peacetreefarm.com
Wholesale greenhouse and plant breeder. Home of the lavenders with trade names Phenomenal and Sensational.

Sage Creations Farm
sagecreationsfarm.com
Offers shipping of more than twenty-five lavender cultivars—many of the plants featured in this book—and makes many more available at the farm location. Sells prebooked custom orders, wholesale and retail.

Takao Nursery
takaonursery.com
Concentrates on California natives, lavender, and drought-tolerant perennials. Sells wholesale and prebooked custom orders.

Tumelo Lavender
tumalolavender.com
Northwest lavender farm offering both retail and wholesale. Offers prebooked customer orders, wholesale and retail.

LAVENDER GROWERS AND FESTIVALS

US Lavender Growers Association
uslavender.org/find-a-supplier
There are numerous lavender farms and nurseries throughout the United States, perhaps close to you. Browse the USLGA member directory for farms and nurseries that sell plants on location.

Norfolk Lavender
norfolk-lavender.co.uk
In the UK, renowned lavender gardens with a farm shop offering lavender plants and products.

Lavender festivals are a great place to find plant starts and get lots of creative ideas for using lavender. Many are hosted by associations or organizations, and some are hosted by individual lavender farms. Search online and you're bound to find something near where you live.
Regional lavender grower groups include the following:

Australian Lavender Growers' Association
talga.com.au

Great Lakes Lavender Growers
greatlakeslavendergrowers.org

Lavender Association of Colorado
coloradolavender.org

Lavender Northwest
lavender-nw.org

New Zealand Lavender Growers Association
lavender.org.nz

Ontario Lavender Association
lavenderontario.org

Sequim Lavender Growers Association
sequimlavendergrowers.com

SOURCES AND RESOURCES

SOME OF MY FAVORITE RESOURCES FOR SCALING UP

BUD CLEANING EQUIPMENT

AT Ferrell
atferrell.com/brand/clipper/equipment
Makes small and large-scale seed cleaners and screens, which work well to clean lavender buds.

COVER CROP SEED
Check out your local feed store or agricultural supply store. Online sources include Territorial Seed Company (territorialseed.com) and High Mowing Organic Seeds (highmowingseeds.com).

CRAFTING SUPPLIES

Afloral
afloral.com/collections/sustainable-floral-supplies
Sustainable floral supplies: metal frogs, environmentally friendly floral foam alternatives, floral chicken wire.

FDC Factory Direct Craft
factorydirectcraft.com/index.php
Large selection of wreath forms, ribbons, and floral design accessories.

Mountain Rose Herbs
mountainroseherbs.com
Large selection of ethically sourced and certified organic essential oils, culinary herbs, and tea herbs.

New Age Floral
newagefloral.com
An EU supplier of Earth-friendly floral products.

DISEASE TESTING

Clemson University Plant and Pest Diagnostic Clinic
clemson.edu/public/regulatory/plant-problem/index.html
Offers phytophthora testing and diagnosis.

ESSENTIAL OIL AND HYDROSOL STILLS

Mile Hi Distilling
milehidistilling.com
Makes small stainless steel moonshine stills with a milk can design. The still that accommodates botanicals like lavender is an affordable option for budding home distillers.

Al-Ambiq
al-ambiq.com/en
Based in Portugal, this company makes beautiful high-quality copper stills of different sizes. You can import directly from the manufacturer or purchase through a regional partner.

Newhouse Manufacturing
newhouse-mfg.com/essential-oil-distillation
Makes food-grade stainless steel stills in a variety of sizes and custom manufactures essential oil distillation equipment for commercial and home use.

ESSENTIAL OIL TESTING

Pyrenessences
pyrenessences.com
A well-regarded independent laboratory located in the French Pyrenees that follows the ISO 17025 standard and provides chromatographic profile analysis of essential oil samples received from around the world.

HAND TOOLS

Zenport Industries
zenportusa.com
Offers a great selection of micro pruners, hand pruners, and sickles. Sells wholesale but website lists authorized dealers.

IRRIGATION AND WATERING SUPPLIES

DripWorks
dripworks.com
Specializes in drip irrigation systems.

MECHANIZED HARVESTERS AND TOOLS

Bizon
bizon-ins.com
Makes several models of harvester specifically designed for lavender as a tractor implement.

HortiHands
hortihands.com
Offers a handheld, walk-behind lightweight harvester specifically made for harvesting lavender and green tea. Its low cost, easy maintenance, and reduced soil compaction make it great for small to medium-size farms.

Spapperi
spapperi.com
An Italian company that makes a semi-automated medicinal herb and lavender harvester.

Tilmor
tilmor.com
Makes hand tools, wheel hoes, walk-behind two-wheel tractors, and four-wheel tractors with a wide range of implements that can cultivate, weed, lay mulch, and seed.

MULCHES, WEED BARRIERS, AND FROST PROTECTION

Johnny's Selected Seeds
johnnyseeds.com
A large offering of different types of weed barriers, including professional landscape fabric and biodegradable paper mulch. Also carries lightweight floating row covers for frost protection.

METRIC CONVERSIONS

US	Metric
1 teaspoon	5 milliliters
1 tablespoon	15 ml
¼ cup	60 ml
⅓ cup	90 ml
½ cup	120 ml
⅔ cup	150 ml
¾ cup	180 ml
1 cup	240 ml

US	Metric
¼ inch	0.6 centimeters
½ in	1.3 cm
1 in	2.5 cm
2 in	5.1 cm
3 in	7.6 cm
4 in	10 cm
5 in	13 cm
10 in	25 cm

US	Metric
1 foot	0.3 meters
2 ft	0.6 m
3 ft	0.9 m
4 ft	1.2 m
5 ft	1.5 m
10 ft	3 m
50 ft	15 m
100 ft	30 m

Acknowledgments

Writing this book has been a pleasure and quite the lavender journey for me, but it would not have happened without the support, wisdom, and generosity of many others.

Thank you—

First to my family, who have each supported me in their own way through my farming and lavender journey. To my husband, Bobby Dery, for being there for me with love, as my sounding board in all things big and small and as my systems man. To Anna and Sophia for understanding my passion and my looming deadlines of all kinds and always cheering me on even if it meant having less time with me. To my mother, Virginia Legarre, who always supported my inquisitiveness, dreams, and drive to follow my heart.

To the lavender pioneers and mentors, Sarah Bader, Andy Van Hevelingen, Tim Upton, Arthur Tucker, and Virginia McNaughton, who inspired me to follow my lavender-growing passion and to better understand this marvelous plant.

To my farming inspirations and old friends Paul Underhill, Tom Willey, and Steve Bennett, who showed me sustainable farming methods and gave me organic farming know-how that I later applied to my lavender growing.

To Lida Lafferty for many years of mentoring and guidance on bee keeping, for being a sounding board for my lavender curiosities, for endless recipe testing with lavender, and for giving me her time to review and test recipes and comment on the culinary chapter of the book.

To Mariana Porras, Juana Porras, and Ignacio Porras, who have been part of the lavender journey from the very beginning, for their hard work and support. Also to Miguel Hernandez, who always contributed to making us better growers with his keen sense of observation and willingness to share throughout the lavender growing season.

To the Colorado Lavender Association founding members, especially Kathy Kimbrough, Carol Schott, Bob Korver, Darrel Sartin, Bob Lane, and Lauri Conner, who I have worked alongside in learning, teaching, and promoting a lavender industry in the state of Colorado.

To Kim Turner for helping me with proofreading and cheering me on through the long nights of editing. To Rebecca Mullen for helping me visualize the process of writing a book.

To Billy Davis for his encouraging words every time I want to create a new lavender field and for guidance with cover cropping and bed forming. To Julie Powell for her creative energy and enthusiasm for all things floral, including floral design and other techniques she has shared and taught to me over the years.

To Andy Van Hevelingen for reviewing the plant descriptions for accuracy and for his willingness to share his wisdom from many years of experience in lavender growing, plant breeding, and research.

To the academic lavender community at Clemson University, for supporting the lavender growers and educating us about phytophthora.

To my main photographer, Kenneth Redding, for his willingness to share his artistry in this book, for capturing the lavender in the early morning light and patiently recording the details of crafting, for being always cheerful and ready to work, and for spreading calm and patience in the room.

To photographer Rob Reece, who was always ready with a camera and coffee in hand to walk the fields in flip flops, always lending his creative expertise with a camera or a drone. To Anna Dery for assisting the photographers and for her creative eye and photographic contributions.

To the Timber Press team for granting me the opportunity and supporting me to write this book about lavender. To editors Tom Fischer, Stacee Lawrence, and Makenna Goodman for believing in me, and to my copy editor, Lorraine Anderson, who would readily pick up the phone and so graciously helped me hash out the small details.

Photo Credits

All photographs by Kenneth Redding with the exception of the following:

Anna Dery, 43, 99, 100, 135 (left, third and bottom),
Danny Delugos, Department of Plant and Environmental Services, Clemson University, 130
Dr. Jeremy Burgess/Science Photo Library, 28
Rob Reece, 14 (bottom), 16, 19, 56, 57, 59 (left), 80, 110, 119–122, 134, 137, 142, 145, 149, 150, 160, 165, 166, 175 (top, left), 235

Alamy
Doris Kindersley ltd, 91

GAP Photos
Abigail Rex, 55 (left)
Dave Zubraski, 66 (right)
Elke Borkowski, 106 (top)
FhF Greenmedia, 104 (bottom)
Fiona Rice, 66 (left)
Graham Strong, 23 (right)
Howard Rice–Cambridge Botanic Gardens, 93
J S Sira, 82, 105 (bottom)
John Glover, 18, 114 (bottom)
Jonathan Buckley, 104 (top)
Juliette Wade, 140
Lynn Keddie, 101 (right)
Mark Turner, 115
Matt Anker, 55 (right), 106 (right)
Nicola Stocken, 22, 101 (left), 189
Nova Photo Graphik, 106 (left), 108, 109
Rob Whitworth, 105 (top)
Suzie Gibbons, 138
Tim Gainey, 103
Visions, 67 (left)

Index

A

Achillea ageratifolia, 114
Agastache foeniculum, 139
Agastache rugosa, 139
Agastache scrophulariifolia, 139
Agastache spp., 136
agritourism, 164–165, 167
Allard's lavender, 109
Aloysia citrodora, 139
amaranth, 137, 218, 240
Amaranthus cruentus, 137
Ammi majus, 137
Anacyclus depressus, 114
anatomy
    bracts / apical bracts, 23, 24, 41, 103, 207
    calyx (bud or sepals), 22–23, 28, 41, 43, 188
    corolla (petals), 22, 41, 43, 188
    cymes, 22, 23, 24
    flower spike, 22–24
    L. angustifolia compared to *L. ×intermedia*, 24–26
    leaves and stems, 24
    oil glands, 23, 28
    variations among species, 24
    verticillasters, 22, 23, 26
    woolly indumentum, 23, 24
Andrews, Susyn, 40
angelica, 141
Angelica archangelica, 141
anise hyssop, 139
annual flowers as companions, 137
Aphelinus abdominalis, 128
aphids / *Aphis* spp., 128, 129, 130
apothecary garden, 20–21
apricot kernel oil, 222
aroma. See scent
aromatherapy, 17, 21, 32
Artemisia spp., 136
autumn home decor, 216–220
autumn sage, 136
AUXIN, 179

B

bachelor's button, 137
balms
    bases, 222
    Peppermint Lavender Balm, 223–225
    topical use cautions, 28, 221
    Winter Solstice Balm, 226
"banana belt" microclimate, 37
basil, 21, 28, 139, 140, 141, 207
bath and body products
    balms, perfumes, and massage oils, 221–226
    creating with hydrosol, 234–235
    mind / body crafts, 158
beardtongue, 136
bee balm 'Gardenview Scarlet', 138
bees, importance of lavender to, 27
Berberis thunbergii, 137
bergamot, 138, 139
bishop's weed, 137
black-eyed Susan, 135, 136
bloom
    agritourism and succession of, 164
    blooming perennial companions, 134–137
    double-blooming cultivars, 48, 164, 217
    extending, 48
    flower color, 41–46
    full bloom, defined, 41–46
    midsummer gap, 27
    stages for harvesting, 144–147
    timing and frequency, 47–50
Bombus species, 27
broom corn, 216, 217, 218, 220
Buddleja davidii, 136
buds
    bud maturity scoring system, 144–147
    crafting buds, 52–53, 162, 175
    fragrant uses for, 158–159
    packaging for added value, 162
    processing for flavoring use, 191–192
    storing, 157
    stripping and cleaning, 154–156
'Buena Vista'
    agritourism use, 164
    best uses of, 52
    bloom timing and frequency, 47, 49
    crafting use, 217, 218
    culinary uses, 138, 204, 206, 207, 209

('Buena Vista' continued)
    fresh and dried colors, compared, 44–45
    plant profile, 63
    propagation, 177
bundles, popular cultivars for dried and fresh-cut, 52–53
butterfly bush, 136
butterfly lavender, 103

C

calendula / *Calendula* spp., 137
calyx (bud or sepals), 22–23, 28, 41, 43, 188
camphor
    as component of essential oil, 27, 28, 30, 31, 83
    cultivars with lower levels of, 83, 189
    scent and, 30, 32, 51, 83
    species / cultivars with high levels of, 189, 231
candle accent, 158
Carex oshimensis 'Everlime', 114
carrier oils, 28, 222
catnip, 139
Centaurea cyanus, 137
Centranthus ruber, 136
Cerastium tomentosum, 136
Chamaemelum nobile, 139
chamomile, 138, 139
chemistry of lavender. See also camphor
    1,8-cineole (eucalyptol), 28, 30, 31, 189
    borneol, 30, 31
    carvacrol, 30
    chemical compounds of flavor and aroma, 191
    cis-beta-ocimene, 30, 31
    coumarin, 32
    ketones, 28, 30
    L. angustifolia 'Twickel Purple' vs. *L. ×intermedia* 'Impress Purple', 31
    lavandulol, 30, 31
    lavandulyl acetate, 30, 31
    linalool, 27, 29, 31, 51, 65, 121, 189, 191
    linalyl acetate, 29, 31, 32, 65, 121, 189, 191
    monoterpenes, 29–30
    phenols, 30
    in specific species, 189–190
    terpenes, 29
    terpinen-4-ol, 30, 189, 191
    thymol, 30
    trans-beta-ocimene, 30, 31
    volatile compounds, 32
chervil, 140, 141
chicken coop, 158
chili peppers, 216, 217, 218, 220
chives, 20, 138
Citrus sinensis, 230
cleaning
    All-Purpose Lavender Cleaner, 230
    My All-Purpose, No-Rinse Floor Cleaner, 231
    using lavender hydrosol, 234
climate, changing, 37, 39
clothes softener, 234
coaster, 159
coconut oil, 222
Cocos nucifera, 222
coir-based growing medium, 180
commercial growing. *See* growing on a larger scale
common lavender, 54
common names, 20, 54, 83, 102
common sage, 28, 141, 218
common wormwood, 136
coneflower, 18, 136, 242
    'Green Twister', 135
confetti, 159
container plantings, 52–53, 103, 124, 138
Coreopsis spp., 136
cornflower, 137
corn poppy, 137
cosmos / Cosmos spp., 137
cover cropping, 132–133
crafting buds, 52–53, 162, 175
crafting products and uses, 163
crafting projects. *See also* balms
    crossover markets and uses, 163
    deodorizing uses, 158, 228
    door swag, 217–220
    easily dried cultivars, 217
    fragrant uses for dried buds, 158–159
    fresh lavender halo, 242–245
    fresh lavender wreath, 236–241
    for the home, 158–159
    inspiration for, 215
    for mind / body use, 158
    products and markets, 163
    sewn, 159
    for special occasions, 159
craspedia, 218

crimson (or scarlet) beebalm, 136, 139
culinary uses. *See also* lavender as a culinary herb
    of essential oils, 190–191
    herb and spice mixes, 204–207
    popular cultivars for, 52–53
    products and markets, 163
cultivars, attributes
    alternatives for unavailable, 51
    bloom timing and frequency, 47–50
    flower color, 41–46
    flowers per cyme, 22
    foliage color, 47
    habit and size, 40
    hardiness, 36–39
    origin, 40
    scent, 51
    spacing, 40–41
    stem length, 40
    uses, 51, 52–53
    variant names, 36
cultivars, listed. *See also* under species names
    'Ana Luisa', 99
    'Anouk', 104
    'Atlas', 103
    'Baby Colby', 164
    'Ballerina' (aka 'Ploughman's Ballerina'), 103, 106
    'Betty's Blue', 44–45, 48, 52, 55, 163, 164, 236
    'Blue Mountain', 44–45
    'Buena Vista' (*See Lavandula angustifolia* 'Buena Vista')
    'Coconut Ice', 44–45, 49, 52, 76
    'Compacta', 54
    'Croxton's Wild', 47, 48, 52, 56, 138, 190, 204
    'Dark Supreme', 44–45, 49, 52, 73
    'Edelweiss', 46, 50, 53, 97, 173, 174, 218, 243
    'Folgate' (*See Lavandula angustifolia* 'Folgate')
    'Folgate Blue', 36
    'Forever Blue', 164, 217
    'French Fields', 44–45, 49, 52, 74
    'Gros Bleu', 24, 46, 50, 53, 84, 97, 189, 231
    'Grosso', 46, 50, 53, 87, 163, 164, 177, 231
    'Hidcote', 20, 21, 22, 54, 114–115, 210
    'Hidcote Giant', 46, 50, 53, 89, 164
    'Hidcote Pink', 44–45, 49, 52, 79, 163, 208
    'Imperial Gem', 44, 45, 49, 52, 64, 138
    'Impress Purple' (*See Lavandula ×intermedia* 'Impress Purple')
    'Irene Doyle', 44–45, 48, 52, 60, 72, 173, 174

'James Compton', 103, 105
'Kew Red' (aka 'Kew Pink', 'Red Kew'), 103, 105
'Lavang 21' (aka Violet Intrigue), 44–45, 48, 52, 61, 163, 164, 217, 236
'Liberty', 103
'Lilac Wings', 103
'Lisa Marie', 100
'Maillette', 33, 44–45, 49, 52, 65, 125, 163, 235
'Melissa' (*See Lavandula angustifolia* 'Melissa')
'Melissa Lilac', 49, 52, 66
'Miss Katherine', 44–45, 47, 49, 52, 81, 204, 205, 208
'Munstead', 54
'Nana Alba', 49, 52, 82, 205
'New Zealand Blue', 44–45
'Niko', 36, 46, 50, 53, 90
'Otto Quast', 103
'Pacific Blue', 49, 52, 67
'Papillon', 103
'Provencal', 103
'Provence', 12, 50, 53, 91, 163, 164, 189, 236
'Purple Bouquet', 48, 52, 62
'Regal Splendour', 104
'Richard Gray', 101
'Riverina Eunice', 44–45
'Riverina Thomas' (*See Lavandula ×intermedia* 'Riverina Thomas')
'Royal Velvet' (*See Lavandula angustifolia* 'Royal Velvet')
'Seal', 50, 53, 93
'Seals Seven Oaks', 23, 44–45
'Sharon Roberts', 49, 52, 69, 189–190
'Super', 46, 50, 53, 83, 94, 163, 177, 236
'SuperBlue', 49, 52, 164
'Thumbelina Leigh', 44–45, 49, 52, 70, 82
'True Munstead', 49, 52, 75
'Tucker's Early Purple', 44, 49, 52, 72
'Twickel Purple', 31, 44, 45
'Vera', 54
'Victory', 103
'Viridis', 37, 103, 104, 106
'Wychoff', 44–45

D

delphinium, 134, 136
Delphinium grandiflora, 136

dianthus, 134
diseases
    alfalfa mosaic virus, 126, 128, 129–130
    fungal and bacterial, 129–130
    phytophthora root and crown rot, 130–131
    spread by pruning, 126
    yellow decline, 129
dog care, 232–233
    Dog Deodorizer and Calming Spray, 233
    Gentle Dog Shampoo, 233
dormancy, 39, 126, 127, 133
dryer bag, 158, 228
dry-roasting buds, 192

E

Echinacea spp., 136
Echinops spp., 136
Eryngium spp., 136
essential oils. *See also* chemistry of lavender
    biological activities, 21
    carrier oils, 28, 222
    cautions, 28, 221, 226
    culinary uses, 190–191
    distilling, 32–33
    judging quality of, 32
    L. ×*intermedia* vs. *L. angustifolia*, 32
    measuring, 227
    popular cultivars for producing, 52–53
    products and markets, 163
    species grown for manufacture of, 21
    topical use, 221
eucalyptol (1,8-cineole), 28, 30, 31, 189
Eunonymus fortunei, 137
European Garden Flora, 36
European Garden Flora (EGF), 36
extraction of buds, 192
extra virgin olive oil, 222

F

fabric mulch, 132, 170
fabric row covers, 133
fennel, 135, 140, 141
fennel seeds, 207

floral uses
    bouquets, 148–149, 216
    fresh flower halo, 242–245
    fresh flower wreath, 236–241
    products and markets, 164
flower color
    clientele preferences, 42
    colored parts, 41
    fresh and dried, compared, 44–46
    RHS color designations, 41–43
Foeniculum vulgare, 141
French lavender, 20, 102, 107
froghoppers, 128

G

Gaillardia spp., 136
garden sage, 136
gas chromatography (GC) test, 32
Genus Lavandula, The (Upson and Andrews), 40
German chamomile, 139
globe thistle, 136
gomphrena, 245
grapeseed oil, 222
grasshoppers (suborder Caelifera), 128–129
Greek oregano, 141, 207
Greek yarrow, 114
green lavender, 103, 106
grinding buds, 192
growing and maintaining. *See also* growing on a larger scale; planting; soil
    choosing a site, 112
    fertilizing, 123–124
    growing zones, 37–39
    as lawn, 12, 114
    pruning, 124–126
    seasonal tasks, 112
    sun requirements, 112
    watering, 121–122
    weed control, 131–133
growing on a larger scale
    countries of growing and production, 18–19
    cultivars that perform well, 162
    design aesthetic and growing philosophy, 162
    designing for access, 165–167
    end goals, 161
    equipment needs, 170

fields, 19, 166 167, 171, 174, 175
intercropping, 165–166
irrigation and long-term maintenance, 165, 174–175
machinery, 166
markets and products, 162–165
other growers as customers, 165
plant selection, 173–174
tillage, 132
yields, 175, 176
growing zones. *See* hardiness

H

hardiness
  choosing the right site, 112
  classifications and zones, 37–38
  cold-hardy species, 54, 83
  as a cultivar attribute, 36–39
  frost-hardy species, 37, 38, 102, 112
  half-hardy species, 37, 38, 107, 112
  tender species, 37, 38, 39, 109, 112, 125
  zones for plant companions, 136–137, 139, 141
harvesting
  bud maturity scoring system, 144–147
  cutting flowers, 144–147
  for dried bundles, 147–148
  drying and storing bundles, 150–153
  for essential oil, 149–150
  for fresh bundles, 144
  for fresh-cut bouquets, 148–149
  preparation for, 143
  screens, 154, 155
  seed cleaner, 154, 155
  stripping and cleaning dried bundles, 154–157
  timing, 144, 147
  tools and materials, 147
Helianthus annuus, 137
Helicrysum italica, 137
herbal tincture, 158
herbes de Provence, 192, 204, 207
herb garden, 140
herbs. *See also* lavender as a culinary herb
  botanically related to lavender, 21
  as companion plants, 140–141
  cultural requirements, 140
  in the mint family, 28
  species grown for herbal use, 21
heterophylla fringed lavender, 109
heterophylla lavender, 109
Hibiscus sabdariffa, 139
Hildegard of Bingen (1098–1179), 20–21
history of lavender, 17–19
holy basil, 139
honeybees, 27
honeysuckle, 137
humidity, 38, 151, 153, 180
hummingbird mint, 136
hydrosol
  defined, 29–30
  in distillation, 33
  popular cultivars for producing, 52–53
  products and markets, 163
  storing, 235
  uses, 163, 234–235
hyssop, 136

I

Ilex paraguariensis, 139
infusing buds, 191–192
insect pests, 128–129
insects, predatory, 129, 130
International Organization for Standardization (ISO), 32
irrigation methods, 122, 174–175

J

Japanese barberry, 114, 137
jojoba oil, 222
Jupiter's beard, 136

K

kitchen garden, 140
Kniphofia spp., 136
Korean mint, 139

L

Lafferty, Lida, 188
lamb's ear, 136
Lamiaceae, 21
landscape uses, 12, 18, 52–53, 114
Latin names, 20
lavandins. *See Lavandula ×intermedia* (aka lavandins)
Lavandula (lavender), 21
Lavandula ×allardii, 37, 38, 109
Lavandula angustifolia
    'Purple Bouquet', 48, 52, 62
Lavandula angustifolia (true lavender), 13
    anatomy compared to L. ×intermedia, 24–26
    aromatherapy use, 21, 32
    bloom timing and frequency, 47–49, 54
    calming effect, 32
    characteristics, 24–25, 54
    common names, 54
    culinary uses, 51, 138, 189–190
    flower as most valuable part, 23–24
    fresh and dried colors, compared, 44–45
    linalool as dominant compound, 29
    phytophthora disease, 130
    planting, 120, 167
    plant profiles, 73–82
    propagation, 177–178
    pruning, 125
    uses for popular cultivars, 52
    yields over five years, 176
Lavandula angustifolia 'Buena Vista'
    agritourism use, 164
    best uses of, 52
    bloom timing and frequency, 47, 49
    crafting use, 217, 218
    culinary uses, 138, 204, 206, 207, 209
    fresh and dried colors, compared, 44–45
    plant profile, 63
    propagation, 177
Lavandula angustifolia 'Folgate'
    best uses of, 52
    bloom timing and frequency, 47, 48
    crossover markets and uses, 162, 163
    culinary uses, 138, 198, 200, 204, 209, 210
    fresh and dried colors, compared, 44–45
    plant profile, 59

Lavandula angustifolia 'Melissa'
    best uses of, 52
    bloom timing and frequency, 49
    crossover markets and uses, 163
    culinary uses, 190, 200, 204, 205, 208
    fresh and dried colors, compared, 44–45
    plant profile, 80
Lavandula angustifolia 'Royal Velvet'
    best uses for, 52
    bloom timing and frequency, 47, 49
    crossover markets and uses, 162, 163, 164
    culinary uses, 189–190, 207, 209, 210
    fresh and dried colors, compared, 44–45
    plant profile, 68
Lavandula angustifolia specific cultivars
    'Baby Colby', 164
    'Betty's Blue', 44–45, 48, 52, 55, 163, 164, 236
    'Blue Mountain', 44–45
    'Coconut Ice', 44–45, 49, 52, 76
    'Compacta', 54
    'Croxton's Wild', 47, 48, 52, 56, 138, 190, 204
    'Dark Supreme', 44–45, 49, 52, 73
    'Forever Blue', 164, 217
    'French Fields', 44–45, 49, 52, 74
    'Hidcote', 20, 21, 22, 54, 114–115, 210
    'Hidcote Pink', 44–45, 49, 52, 79, 163, 208
    'Imperial Gem', 44, 45, 49, 52, 64, 138
    'Irene Doyle', 44–45, 48, 52, 60, 72, 173, 174
    'Lavang 21' (aka Violet Intrigue), 44–45, 48, 52, 61, 163, 164, 217, 236
    'Maillette', 33, 44–45, 49, 52, 65, 125, 163, 235
    'Melissa Lilac', 49, 52, 66
    'Miss Katherine', 44–45, 47, 49, 52, 81, 204, 205, 208
    'Munstead', 54
    'Nana Alba', 49, 52, 82, 205
    'New Zealand Blue', 44–45, 59
    'Pacific Blue', 49, 52, 67
    'Riverina Eunice', 44–45
    'Seals Seven Oaks', 23, 44–45
    'Sharon Roberts', 49, 52, 69, 189–190
    'SuperBlue', 49, 52, 164
    'Thumbelina Leigh', 44–45, 49, 52, 70, 82
    'True Munstead', 49, 52, 75
    'Tucker's Early Purple', 44–45, 49, 52, 72
    'Twickel Purple', 31, 44, 45
    'Vera', 54
    'Wychoff', 44–45

Lavandula ×*chaytorae*
    plant profiles, 99–101
    traits, 98
Lavandula ×*chaytorae* specific cultivars
    'Ana Luisa', 99
    'Lisa Marie', 100
    'Richard Gray', 101
Lavandula dentata, 37, 38, 107–108, 124–125, 189
Lavandula dentata var. *candicans*, 107
Lavandula dentata var. *dentata*, 107
Lavandula ×*heterophylla*, 37, 109
Lavandula ×*intermedia* (aka lavandins), 14
    anatomy compared to *L. angustifolia*, 24–26
    bloom timing and frequency, 47, 50
    bouquet use, 32, 83, 173
    characteristics, 24, 26, 83
    colors, fresh and dried, 46
    common names, 83
    flower as most valuable part, 23–24
    hydrosol, 234
    invigorating effect, 32
    lavandins as companion plants, 136–137
    planting, 120, 167
    plant profiles, 84–97
    propagation, 177–178, 183
    pruning, 124–126
    therapeutic uses of compounds, 27, 30–31
    uses for popular cultivars, 53
    wilt resistance, 33
    yields over five years, 176
Lavandula ×*intermedia* 'Impress Purple'
    best uses of, 53
    bloom timing and frequency, 47, 50
    chemical constituents, 31, 231
    crafting use, 217, 236, 243
    crossover markets and uses, 162, 163, 164
    dried bundles, 153
    as high-camphor, 231
    plant profile, 88
    propagation, 177
Lavandula ×*intermedia* 'Riverina Thomas'
    best uses of, 53
    bloom timing and frequency, 47, 50
    colors, fresh and dried, 46
    crafting use, 217, 218, 236
    crossover markets and uses, 163, 164
    as a high-camphor cultivar, 231
    large scale growing of, 173, 174

    plant profile, 92
Lavandula ×*intermedia* specific cultivars
    'Edelweiss', 46, 50, 53, 97, 173, 174, 218, 243
    'Gros Bleu', 24, 46, 50, 53, 84, 97, 189, 231
    'Grosso', 46, 50, 53, 87, 163, 164, 177, 231
    'Hidcote Giant', 46, 50, 53, 89, 164
    'Niko', 36, 46, 50, 53, 90
    'Provence', 12, 50, 53, 91, 163, 164, 189, 236
    'Seal', 50, 53, 93
    'Super', 46, 50, 53, 83, 94, 163, 177, 236
Lavandula lanata, 37, 189
Lavandula latifolia (spike lavender), 21, 28, 37, 83, 109
Lavandula pedunculata, 37, 103, 104
Lavandula pterostoechas, 37, 38
Lavandula stoechas
    apical bracts, 23, 41, 103
    aroma and taste, 189
    bloom time, 47
    characteristics, 102–103
    chemical compounds in, 189
    common names, 20, 102
    as a container plant, 102, 103
    flower spike, 22, 23
    history, 102
    ornamental use, 24
    plant profiles, 104–107
    propagation, 177
    pruning, 124–125
    subspecies and hybrids, 103
Lavandula stoechas specific cultivars
    'Anouk', 104
    'Kew Red', 103
    'Liberty', 103
    'Lilac Wings', 103
    'Otto Quast', 103
    'Provencal', 103
    'Regal Splendour', 104
    'Victory', 103
    'Viridis', 103
Lavandula stoechas subsp. *pedunculata*, 103, 105
    'Atlas', 103
    'James Compton', 103, 105
    'Papillon', 103
Lavandula stoechas subsp. *stoechas* f. *rosea* 'Kew Red' (aka 'Kew Pink', 'Red Kew'), 103, 105
Lavandula stoechas ×*viridis* 'Ballerina' (aka 'Ploughman's Ballerina'), 103, 106

Lavandula viridis (aka green lavender; *Lavandula stoechas* 'Viridis'), 37, 103, 104, 106
lavandulyl acetate, 30, 31
lavender as a culinary herb
    complementary ingredients and fruits, 191
    floral and spice notes, 187–188
    food partners, 188
    species to cook with, 188–190
    using in moderation, 187–188
lavender flavor, methods of adding. See also recipes
    compound butters, 212–213
    extracts and bitters, 202–203
    herb and spice mixes, 192, 204–207
    infusing, extracting, and grinding buds, 191–192
    pairing with chocolate, 198–201
    pepper mill grinder recipes, 208–209
    sugars and syrups, 194–197
    tools for, 193
lawn, 12, 114
Legarre, Paola
    book overview, 15
    path to growing lavender, 9, 12–15
    portrait, 10
lemon balm, 138, 139
lemon beebalm, 139
lemon bergamot, 139
lemons, 206, 210–211
lemon thyme, 140, 141, 213
lemon verbena, 139
limonene, 30, 31
Lippia graveolens, 141
Lonicera caprifolium, 137

M

marigold, 217, 218, 242
marjoram / sweet marjoram, 28, 140, 141
markets and products, 162–165
massage oils, 222
Matricaria recutita, 139
medicinal uses, 20–21, 102
Melissa officinalis, 139
Mentha ×piperita, 139
Mentha spicata, 139
Mentha suaveolens, 139
Mexican hat, 136
Mexican oregano, 141

microclimates, 37
mind / body crafting projects, 158
mint family (Lamiaceae), 21, 28, 29
mints
    apple mint, 139
    peppermint, 28, 138, 139, 223
    pineapple mint, 138, 139
    spearmint, 28, 139
Monarda citriodora, 139
Monarda didyma, 136, 139
Monarda fistulosa, 139
Mount Atlas daisy, 114
Mrs. Burns lemon basil, 139
mulch, 132, 133, 157, 170

N

neck wrap, 159
Nepeta cataria, 139
nitrogen, 123
Nosema locustae, 129
nutrients, 123

O

Ocimum basilicum, 141
Ocimum ×citriodorum, 139
Ocimum tenuiflorum, 139
Olea europaea, 222
Oriental poppy, 136
Origanum heracleoticum, 141
Origanum majorana, 141
Origanum syriacum, 141
Oswego tea, 139

P

Papaver orientale, 136
Papaver rhoeas, 137
parasitoid wasp, 128
peat moss, 180
peduncles, 24
pencil holder, 158
Penstemon spp., 136
perennial companions, 134–137

perennials, blooming, 134–137
perennials, low growing, 114
perfumes, 22, 222
perlite, 180
petals, 22, 41
pH, 113, 116
Philaenus spumarius, 128
phosphorous, 123
Physica (Hildegard of Bingen), 20–21
Phytophthora nicotianae, 130, 131
phytophthora / *Phytophthora*, 130–131
planting
    different hardiness groups, 38
    how to plant, 111, 118–120
    lavenders treated as annuals, 38
    spacing, 120
    timing, 117–118
planting, larger scale
    design and spacing, 170–171
    designing for access, 165–167
    equipment needs, 170
    planting layouts, 167–169
    planting process, 170–172
    plant selection, 173–174
    soil and field preparation, 171–172
planting companions
    annual flowers, 137
    blooming perennials, 134–137
    kitchen herbs, 140–141
    lavender lawn companions, 114
    shrubs and vines, 137
    tea herbs, 138–139
plant selection, 35–36, 173–174
pollinators and lavender
potassium, 123
prairie coneflower, 136
products and markets, 162–165
propagation
    advantages of, 176
    cross-pollination, 103, 177
    from cuttings, 177–180
    growing from seed, 177
    keys to success, 178–179, 184
    plant patents and, 178
    seasons for, 176, 178
    sports (mutations), 177
    step-by-step, 181–185
    terminology, 179

pruning, 124–126
Prunus armeniaca, 222
purple giant hyssop, 139

Q

Queen Anne's lace, 137

R

Ratibida Columnifera, 136
recipes
    Alcohol-Free Lavender Extract, 202
    Cherry Tomatoes with Goat Cheese, Olive Oil, and Herbes de Provence, 207
    Chocolate Lavender Shortbread with Sea Salt, 201
    compound butters, 212–213
    Ground Lavender Sugar, 195
    Herbes de Provence, 207
    Infused Lavender Sugar, 194, 195
    Lavender and Lemongrass Bitters, 203
    Lavender Chili Spice Mix, 204
    Lavender Cocoa, 194, 198
    Lavender Extract, 202
    Lavender Honey, 196
    Lavender Hot Cocoa Mix, 198
    Lavender Lemon Pepper, 204, 206
    Lavender Rosemary Salt, 209
    Lavender Vanilla Sugar, 196
    Pink Fusion Lavender Rainbow Salt, 208
    Preserved Lemons with Lavender, Black Peppercorns, Star Anise, and Thyme, 210
    Simple Lavender Syrup, 194, 197
red hot poker, 136
red orache, 18
Roman chamomile, 139
rooting hormone, 179
roselle, 139
rosemary
    chemical composition, 30
    as herb companion, 141
    pairing with lavender, 140, 191, 204, 209, 212
    in a tea garden, 138
Rosmarinus officinalis, 141
row covers, floating, 133

Royal Horticultural Society (RHS)
    Colour Chart, 41–43
    growing zones classification system, 36–37
rudbeckia / *Rudbeckia* spp., 134, 136

S

sachets, 158, 158, 228–229
Sage Creations, 12–14
Salvia greggii, 136
Salvia officinalis, 136, 141
Salvia ×*sylvestris*, 136
Satureja hortensis, 141
Satureja montana, 141
scent
    chemical compounds, 29, 51, 191
    in consumer products, 17
    as a cultivar attribute, 51
    fragrant uses for dried lavender, 158–159
    true lavender vs. spike lavender, 83
scented gifts, 221–226
sedum, 18
Sedum spp., 136
sepals. *See* calyx
Shirley poppy, 137
Simmondsia chinensis, 222
snow in summer, 136
soap, 158
soil
    nutrients, 123–124
    percolation test, 116
    pH, 113, 116
    preparing for large-scale planting, 171–172
soil analysis, 116
soilless growing medium, 178, 180
Spanish lavender, 20, 102, 107
species
    by hardiness group, 37–38
    Latin and common names, 20
    variations from genetic mutations, 177
Spike It with Lavender: Recipes for Living (Lafferty), 188
spike lavender, 21, 28, 30, 83
spittlebugs, 128
Stachys byzantina, 136

stems
    debudding, 154–156
    in fresh-cut bouquets, 148
    in lavender anatomy, 24
    length, 40
    long and dramatic, 83
    nutrient requirements, 123
    using discarded, 157
stoechas, 102
Stolbur phytoplasma, 129
stonecrop, 136
summer savory, 140, 141
sunflower, 135, 137
Syrian oregano, 141

T

tea garden plants, 138–139
temperatures
    cold temperatures, withstanding, 54, 83
    fall vs. spring, 118
    freeze dates, 39
    lavenders in four hardiness groups, 38, 112
    low temperature tolerance range, 37, 38
    plants in full sun, 112
    protecting against extreme, 39, 123, 133
    USDA plant hardiness map, 36
    watering and, 121
throw pillow, 159
thyme, 141, 189, 190, 191, 210, 212, 213, 240
thymol, 30
Thymus ×*citriodorus*, 141
Thymus vulgaris, 141
tickseed, 136
Trifolium repens, 174
true lavender. *See Lavandula angustifolia* (aka true lavender)
Tucker, Arthur, 54
tulsi, 139

U

Upson, Tim, 40
USDA (US Department of Agriculture)
    hardiness zones
        bloom time and, 47–48

identifying your zone, 47
low temperature tolerance ranges, 37
for plant companions, 136–137, 139, 141
plant hardiness zone map, 36
US Patent and Trademark Office (USPTO), 178

wild bergamot, 138, 139
wild marjoram, 27, 218, 240
wilt resistance, 83
wintercreeper, 137
winter protection, 133
winter savory, 140, 141
wood sage, 136
wreath, 236–241

V

vermiculite, 180
Violet Intrigue, 61, 163, 164
Vitis vinifera, 222

Y

yarrow, 114, 134, 135, 136, 218, 220, 240, 245
yerba mate, 139

W

wedding toss, 159
weed fabric, 175
white clover, 174

Z

za'atar, 141
zinnia, 137, 216, 218
Zinnia elegans, 137

About the Author

PAOLA LEGARRE has been passionate about gardening since she was a child and has worked in organic farming since 1995. Her studies in development and agricultural economics at UC Berkeley and food and agribusiness at the University of Santa Clara inspired her to pursue her farming and marketing interests further, eventually leading her to start her own farm, Sage Creations, where she first planted lavender in 2006. As her lavender fields grew, Paola extended her product line to include essential oil, bath and body products, dried flowers, and lavender plant starts. She has been trialing different species and cultivars of lavender to see which are best suited to the Colorado climate and its different zones. The farm now has more than six acres in lavender production and grows and propagates four species and more than sixty different cultivars of lavender.

Besides lavender fields, Paola's small-scale, high-intensity farm has medicinal and culinary herb crops, cut-flower gardens, heirloom vegetable plots, and a cherry orchard. Her farm uses sustainable farming practices: nourishing soil life, avoiding herbicides and synthetic fertilizers, rotating plantings with cover crops, and encouraging pollinators and beneficial insects through diversified plant hedgerows, companion planting, and insect releases.

Through Sage Creations, Paola teaches workshops and classes and has mentored many lavender growers and home gardeners through the years. She is a founding member of the Colorado Lavender Association and has presented at workshops and conferences across the United States, including the US Lavender Growers Association conference. Paola and her Sage Creations Farm have been featured in regional and national publications and on television and radio, including on PBS and Colorado Public Radio.

Paola lives and farms with her husband and two children in Palisade, Colorado. Her love of plants and growing things, as well as her love of teaching and sharing her knowledge and farming experience, inspired her to write this book.

About the Photographer

KENNETH REDDING picked up his first camera while in high school in Southern California and has been taking pictures for more than thirty years. Ken's love of the outdoors drew him to Colorado, where he now lives with his wife, Camille, and their two Australian shepherds. He has captured images of people, landscapes, and buildings inside and out for a wide range of clients, including the Nature Conservancy, the North Face, the Colorado Tourism Office, *Cooking Light* magazine, *Newsweek*, and *Time*. His unique style of photography is on display on his website, kenreddingphotography.com.